Voyages Through Space and Time

Voyages Through Space and Time

Jon K. Wooley

Eastern Michigan University

Wadsworth Publishing Company
Belmont, California
A Division of Wadsworth, Inc.

Astronomy Editor: Anne Scanlan-Rohrer
Editorial Assistant: Leslie With
Production Editor: Carol Lombardi
Managing Designer: Stephen Rapley
Print Buyer: Barbara Britton
Permissions Editor: Jeanne Bosschart
Copy Editor: Charles Hibbard
Cover photo by Voyager 1—NASA/JPL
Cover Design: Annette Scheid
Signing Representative: Dave Leach
Printer: Malloy Lithographing

This book is printed on acid-free paper that meets Environmental Protection Agency standards for recycled paper.

1 2 3 4 5 6 7 8 9 10—96 95 94 93 92

ISBN 0-534-17226-1

CONTENTS

Chapter 7 125

Phases And Eclipses

Chapter 8 159

Planetary Phases and Motions

Chapter 9   191

Satellite and Ring Systems

Chapter 10   209

Magnitudes and the H-R Diagram

Appendices   227

Ordering *Voyager* Software   256

PREFACE

Voyages Through Space and Time is the first laboratory manual to use the the power of desktop computers to create an innovative, motivating learning experience for astronomy students. It requires a Macintosh computer and *Voyager, The Interactive Desktop Planetarium* software.

Organization of This Manual

The first three chapters contain introductory astronomical information; following chapters contain projects and exercises that help students explore the skies, via the *Voyager* software, and understand what they see.

  •Chapter 1 discusses the geocentric and heliocentric theories and the laws of Kepler and Newton.
  •Chapter 2 describes the horizon and equatorial coordinate systems.
  •Chapter 3 covers various types of time.
  •Chapters 4–10 contain groups of projects that allow students—by observing, measuring, recording, and drawing their own conclusions—to practice real hands-on astronomy.

Goals—from understanding sidereal time to collecting physical data on planets to predicting lunar eclipses—are clearly set out for each project. Each project consists of an introduction to the topic to be investigated, instructions on entering information and commands required by the *Voyager* program, the types of observations or measurements to be made, and questions to be answered. Most projects require an average of one or two hours to complete and are sufficiently self-contained so they can be sequenced in almost any order.

Projects from *Voyages Through Space and Time* could replace or supplement the more traditional astronomy labs that are usually part of college astronomy courses. They might be required assignments or extra credit homework in lecture sections. The chart on pages xiv–xv cross-references each project to several introductory astronomy texts, so the exercises can be more easily integrated with other classwork.

About the Software

When Carina Software introduced *Voyager, The Interactive Desktop Planetarium* in 1988, the program got rave reviews and was ranked as one of the top educational programs of 1989. Extensive use of *Voyager* in the introductory astronomy classes at Eastern Michigan University has demonstrated its potential for changing the way astronomy is taught and learned.

Voyager is called a desktop planetarium because it duplicates many features of a more traditional planetarium. Even after adding the cost of a Macintosh computer and a high quality projection device for classroom demonstrations, *Voyager* is considerably less expensive than a traditional planetarium. In many ways it is even better.

Because of the vast distances and long time spans involved it is difficult, if not impossible, for the average individual to observe many of the most basic and interesting astronomical phenomena. In an instructional setting, insufficient observing equipment and staff, often combine with cloudy and light polluted skies to make evening observing sessions impractical. With *Voyager,* time and space can be compressed and manipulated—and the sky is always dark and cloudless.

Voyager places the sky under the user's control. Students can interact with the program in numerous ways, making observations and taking measurements. They can view the sky from virtually any place in the solar system and at any time past, present, or future. Simple menu selections move the user from ancient Athens to present day Paris, Moscow, or Mars. One can watch the Moon go through its phases, track the Sun and planets as the move along the zodiac, predict lunar and solar eclipses, watch the Galilean moons revolve about Jupiter, or just learn the constellations. What took astronomers centuries to discover students can do in a matter of a few hours. The sky really is the limit with Voyager!

At the heart of the program is a celestial database of 14,000 objects/including 9,100 stars, 3,000 deep sky objects such as galaxies and nebulae, 1,600 binary stars, 160 variable stars, the Sun, Moon, and planets. A click of the mouse identifies any of these objects, and one can zoom in for a closer look or for distance, temperature, size, or rising and setting times. Pertinent information such as location, time, and sky coordinates are displayed and updated. Scrollbars let you move quickly to different parts of the sky (Figure Pl.l).

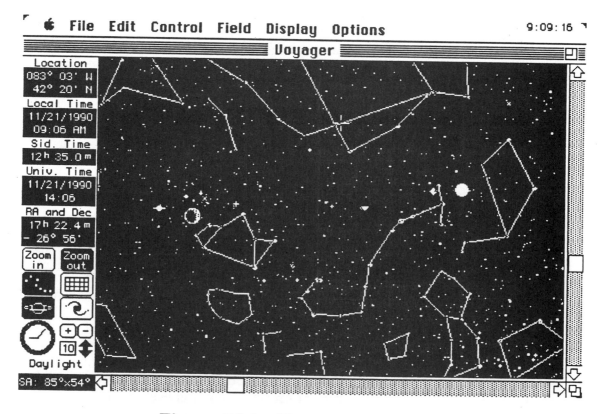

Figure P1.1 Voyager Screen

Student Responses

Voyager's sophistication and ease of use seem to intrigue and motivate students. Not only are they learning more about astronomy and scientific investigation, they are also learning a great deal about computers.

It is refreshing to see enthusiastic and positive reactions such as the following:

> This program is obviously very sophisticated. The possibilities are incredible. Familiarity with the *Voyager* program offers an exciting and easy way to learn astronomy at your own pace, time, and level of ability.

> It is a valuable learning tool. It helps get you used to working with computers as well as teaching you astronomy the way it should be taught.

> Very interesting and fun. I am looking forward to future projects.

> I was initially intimidated by the whole idea of using a computer. Still, in less than ten minutes, I had embarked on a journey aboard *Voyager*. It was an intriguing project.

Working through the projects in *Voyages Through Space and Time* is only a beginning—an introduction to the fascinating world of modern astronomy and microcomputing. Many more projects can be imagined. As students progress through the text, they will undoubtedly think of new projects to do and new questions to ask. These vital activities—asking questions and finding answers—are as important to individual learning as they are to science itself.

Acknowledgments

I would like to express my appreciation to Carina Software for the superlative job they have done in writing the *Voyager* program. It should be noted that a number of the illustrations in this text, such as Figure Pl.l, are "screen dumps" from the software.

I also extend my thanks to one of my students, David Bush, who spent a great deal of time reading and doing the projects. Many of his suggestions and ideas have been incorporated in this text. I also extend my gratitude to colleagues who provided valuable insights during the development stages of this project: Bruce Bailick, University of Washington; Kenneth T. Broun, Jr., Tidewater Community College; Leo Connolly, California Sate University, San Bernardino; and Peter Schull, Oklahoma State University.

Last but not least I would like to thank all of the astronomy students whose enthusiasm and comments have made writing *Voyages Through Space and Time* not only possible but enjoyable as well.

Jon K.Wooley
Department of Physics and Astronomy
Eastern Michigan University

CROSS REFERENCE

Key to Chapters in Introductory Astronomy Texts

The following chart cross-references the projects in this book to chapters in the major introductory astronomy texts listed below.

Seeds, *Horizons: Exploring the Universe*
    Wadsworth Publishing Company, 1991 Edition

Seeds, *Foundations of Astronomy*
    Wadsworth Publishing Company, 1990 Edition

Hartmann, *Astronomy: The Cosmic Journey*
    Wadsworth Publishing Company, 1991 Edition

Hartmann, *The Cosmic Voyage Through Time and Space*
    Wadsworth Publishing Company

Abell, Morris, Wolff, *Exploration of the Universe*
    Saunders College Publishing, Sixth Edition, 1991

Kaufmann, *The Universe*
    W. H. Freeman and Company, Third Edition, 1991

Kaufmann, *Discovering the Universe*
    W. H. Freeman and Company, Second Edition, 1990

Zeilik, *Astronomy: The Evolving Universe*
    John Wiley & Sons, Inc., Sixth Edition, 1991

Flower, *Understanding the Universe*
    West Publishing Company, First Edition, 1990

Kuhn, *Astronomy: A Journey into Science*
    West Publishing Company, First Edition, 1989

Pasachoff, *Astronomy: From Earth to the Universe*
    Saunders College Publishing, Fourth Edition, 1991

Morrison and Wolff, *Frontiers of Astronomy*
    Saunders College Publishing, Fourth Edition, 1990

Voyages Through Space and Time Project (page)	Seeds *Horizons: Exploring the Universe*	Seeds *Foundations of Astronomy*	Hartmann *Astronomy: The Cosmic Journey*	Hartmann *The Cosmic Voyage*	Abell, Morris, Wolff *Exploration of the Universe*	Kaufmann *The Universe*
Project 1 (37) Voyager 1.2						
Project 2 (47) The Horizon System			1 Essay B	1 Essay B	1, 5 App 6	2
Project 3 (55) Constellations and Planets	2	2	1	1	1	2
Project 4 (63) The Equatorial System	2, 3 App B	App A	Essay B	Essay B	1, 5 App 6	2
Project 5 (75) The Inner Planets	3, 4, 17	2, 4, 21	3, 8	3, 8	2 App 7	4
Project 6 (83) The Outer Planets	3, 4, 18	2, 4, 22	3	3	2 App 7	4
Project 7 (89) Precession	3	2	2	2	4	2
Project 8 (99) The Earth's Seasons	3	2	1	1	5	2
Project 9 (107) Types of Time	App B	App A	Essay B	Essay B	5	2
Project 10 (115) The Equation of Time		App A				2
Project 11 (121) Sidereal Time	App B	App A			5	2
Project 12 (127) Lunar Phases	3	3	7	7	1, 6	3
Project 13 (135) Conjunctions					6	
Project 14 (141) Lunar Eclipses	3	3	1	1	6	3
Project 15 (149) Solar Eclipses	3	3	1	1	6	3
Project 16 (161) Planetary Phases	4	4			2	4
Project 17 (169) Mercury and Venus					2	4
Project 18 (175) Retrograde Motion	4	4	3		1	4
Project 19 (185) View from Mars						
Project 20 (193) Jupiter's Moons	4	5	3, 11	3, 11	2, 17	4, 14
Project 21 (203) Planetary Rings	18	22, 23	12	12	17	15, 16
Project 22 (211) Magnitude Systems	2, 8	2, 9	16	16	7, 22	19
Project 23 (219) Spectral Classes and the H-R Diagram	6, 8	7, 9	17	17	22, 24	19

Voyages Through Space and Time Project (page)	Kaufmann *Discovering the Universe*	Zeilik *Astronomy: The Evolving Universe*	Flower *Understanding the Universe*	Kuhn *Astronomy: A Journey into Science*	Pasachoff *Astronomy: From Earth to the Universe*	Morrison and Wolff *Frontiers of Astronomy*
Project 1 (37) Voyager 1.2						
Project 2 (47) The Horizon System	2	1	1, 2	Prologue	5	1
Project 3 (55) Constellations and Planets	2	1		1	5	
Project 4 (63) The Equatorial System	2	1	2	1 App D	5	1
Project 5 (75) The Inner Planets	3,7	3, 9, 10	2, 3, 6, 7	2, 3, 5, 7, 8	3, 6	2
Project 6 (83) The Outer Planets	3,8	3, 11	2, 3, 8	3, 5, 7, 9	3, 6	2
Project 7 (89) Precession	2	1	5	6	5	
Project 8 (99) The Earth's Seasons	2		2	1	5	3
Project 9 (107) Types of Time			1		5	
Project 10 (115) The Equation of Time					5	
Project 11 (121) Sidereal Time			1		5	
Project 12 (127) Lunar Phases	2	1	2	1	6	4
Project 13 (135) Conjunctions					2	
Project 14 (141) Lunar Eclipses	2	1	2	6	6	4
Project 15 (149) Solar Eclipses	2	1	2	6	6	4
Project 16 (161) Planetary Phases	3	1	2, 3	1, 3	3	1
Project 17 (169) Mercury and Venus	3	1	2	2	3	1
Project 18 (175) Retrograde Motion	3	1, 2, 3	2, 3	1	3	
Project 19 (185) View from Mars						
Project 20 (193) Jupiter's Moons	3	4, 11	3, 8, 9	3	3, 12	1, 6
Project 21 (203) Planetary Rings	8	11	8,9	9	13, 14 15	6
Project 22 (211) Magnitude Systems	12	14	14	14	21	8
Project 23 (219) Spectral Classes and the H-R Diagram	12	14	13, 14	14	20, 21 22	10

CHAPTER 1

The Motions of Celestial Objects

THE HELIOCENTRIC THEORY

The Sun is an average star of small significance in the overall scheme of the universe but is of central importance to our immediate neighborhood of space, the **solar system**. It sends life-supporting energy to the Earth and its gravitational force dictates the motions of nine planets and numerous smaller objects such as asteroids and comets. While only average compared to many stars, the Sun is more than 100 times the size of the Earth and many times larger than Jupiter, the largest of all planets.

The Sun's family of objects move around it in **elliptical** orbits of varying shape and size. In order of increasing distance from the Sun the planets are Mercury, Venus, the Earth, Mars, Jupiter, Saturn, Uranus, Neptune, and Pluto. The four inner planets together with Pluto are often referred to as **terrestrial planets** because of their similarity to the Earth, and the four remaining planets are frequently called **Jovian planets** since in many ways they resemble Jupiter. From the closest planet, Mercury, to the most distant planet, Pluto, the solar system extends some 5,914 million kilometers. At even larger distances the remote realm of the comets defines the outer reaches of the solar system.

All of the planets revolve about the Sun in the same direction as the Earth and in very nearly the same plane. The Earth's orbital plane is known as the **ecliptic plane** and the time required to orbit the Sun is called the **sidereal period of revolution**. For the Earth this period is one year but each planet has a different period of revolution. Mercury takes only 88 days while distant Pluto requires 248.5 years to make its journey around the Sun!

As planets revolve around the Sun they also rotate, and the distinction between these terms should be noted. **Revolution** always refers to the motion of one object about another object whereas **rotation** relates to the motion of a single object about an imaginary axis passing through it. The Earth's **sidereal period of rotation** is what is commonly called one day. The Earth rotates 365 1/4 times as it revolves once around the Sun. Some planets have periods of rotation that are longer then the Earth's and some have rotational periods that are shorter. Strangely enough, the largest planet, Jupiter, rotates once in a little less than ten hours while little Mercury takes more then 58 days.

The acceptance of this Sun-centered picture, called the **heliocentric theory**, is the result of centuries of scientific thought and observations. One of the first advocates of the heliocentric theory was the Greek astronomer Aristarchus, who lived about 300 B.C. However, it was not until centuries later that the Polish astronomer Copernicus revived and revised the ancient idea of a Sun-centered system. His heliocentric theory was published in a book called *De Revolutionibus* (Concerning the Revolutions) in 1543 A.D., the year of his death.

It was more than 60 years later that the first accurate description of planetary motion was made by the German astronomer Johannes Kepler. Between 1609 and 1618 Kepler, using the observations of the Danish astronomer Tycho Brahe, discovered three laws that describe planetary motion. The first two laws were published in the book *Commentaries on the Motions of Mars* in 1609; the third appeared in a 1618 book called *The Harmony of the Worlds*.

Kepler's Laws of Planetary Motion

FIRST LAW: Each planet moves about the Sun in an elliptical orbit with the Sun at one focus.

SECOND LAW: The line connecting the Sun and a planet sweeps out equal areas in equal intervals of time.

THIRD LAW: The semi-major axis cubed is equal to the period of revolution squared.

Kepler's laws are a significant departure from earlier heliocentric theories which had planets orbiting the Sun in circular orbits. Kepler discarded the circles and replaced them with ellipses. Whereas all circles have the same shape but can differ in size, ellipses can differ in both shape and size. The size of a circle is given by its radius. The **size** of an ellipse is specified by its **semi-major axis**, which is one-half of the **major axis** (see Figure 1.1). The semi-major axis is usually designated by "a".

The **shape** of an ellipse is specified by the **eccentricity**, which can be defined as the ratio, cf/a, where cf is the distance between the center of the ellipse and the focus. All circles have eccentricities equal to 0. For ellipses, eccentricities are always greater than 0 but less than 1. If the eccentricity is equal to 0 the ellipse is, in fact, a circle but as the eccentricity approaches 1 the ellipse becomes more and more elongated in appearance.

Kepler discovered that planet orbits have eccentricities very close to but not exactly equal to 0. That is, the orbits are very nearly circular. Were it not for the accurate observations of Tycho Brahe, Kepler would not have been able to discover the planets' small deviations from circular motion.

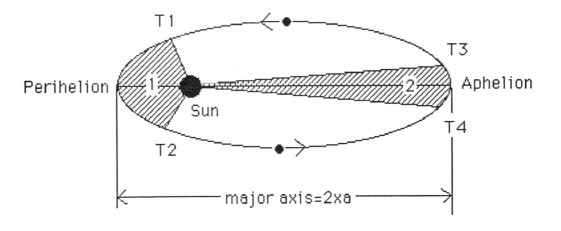

Figure 1.1   Kepler's Laws

Because a planet moves around the Sun in an elliptical orbit with the Sun at one focus, its distance from the Sun continually changes. When a planet is closest to the Sun it is said to be at **perihelion** and when it is farthest from the Sun, at **aphelion**. On the average, however, a planet's distance from the Sun is equal to the semi-major axis of its elliptical orbit. For the Earth this distance is approximately 93 million miles.

Kepler's second law says that if the time required for a planet to move from T1 to T2 in Figure 1.1 is the same as the time from T4 to T3, then the areas swept out must be equal; area 1 must equal area 2. This law requires that as a planet's distance from the Sun changes, so must its orbital speed. A planet moves fastest when it is closest to the Sun at the perihelion point and slowest when it is farthest from the Sun at the aphelion point.

Kepler's third law states that the cube of a planet's sidereal period of revolution, P, is equal to the square of its semi-major axis, that is,

$$a^3 = P^2$$

In the above equation the sidereal period, P, must be expressed in years. The semi-major axis, a, must be expressed in terms of a unit of distance called the **astronomical unit** (AU). One astronomical unit is defined as the Earth's average distance from the Sun. Thus, it is the semi-major axis of the Earth and is equivalent to 93 million miles. In terms of this unit Mercury is 0.39, the Earth is 1.0, Jupiter is 5.2, and Pluto is 39.5 astronomical units from the Sun. The third law indicates that the periods of revolution increase with increasing distance from the Sun. Mercury's sidereal period is 0.24 years (88 days), while Pluto's is 248.5 years.

Kepler's laws describe how planets move but do not explain why they move in the way they do. Neither Kepler nor his friend Galileo, who in 1609 first used the telescope for astronomical observation, could answer the question "why?". The answer was found by the Englishman Isaac Newton, who during 1666 and 1667 discovered the force called gravity. Newton explained planetary motion in terms of the gravitational forces acting between the Sun and planets and demonstrated that Kepler's laws are a natural consequence of gravity.

Newton's **Universal Law of Gravity** asserts that the gravitational force attracting any two objects varies directly as the product of their masses and inversely as the square of the distance between them.

The law is written as

$$F = \frac{GmM}{D^2}$$

where D is the distance between the masses m and M, and G is a number called the universal gravitational constant.

The force of gravity rapidly decreases as the distance between the two masses increases. For example, Pluto at 40 astronomical units from the Sun experiences a gravitational force that is 1,600 times smaller than the force at the Earth's distance. Yet, an object would have to be infinitely far from the Sun to feel no pull from the Sun's gravity! In fact, every object in the universe attracts every other object according to Newton's law. The Sun, the solar system, our galaxy, and the universe are all held together by the glue of gravity.

In the same year that he discovered the law of gravity Newton proposed three general laws of motion.

Newton's Laws of Motion

FIRST LAW: An object at rest remains at rest and an object moving in a straight line at a constant speed continues to do so unless acted upon by an unbalanced force.

SECOND LAW: Force (F) is equal to mass (M) times acceleration (A). That is, **F=M x A**

THIRD LAW: For every force there is an equal but opposite force.

These three laws can be used to accurately predict the motions of objects in the universe.

Newton's insight was the culmination of centuries of speculation, thought, and observation. But he himself pointed out, "if I have seen farther than others it is because I have stood on the shoulders of giants." By this he meant that he could not have discovered his laws had it not been for the work done by such individuals as Copernicus, Brahe, Kepler, and Galileo.

THE GEOCENTRIC THEORY

The heliocentric theory is not only correct, it is also easy to visualize. Everyone can imagine standing outside the solar system watching the planets as they move around the Sun. Although this theory was first proposed as early as 300 B.C., most astronomers up until the time of Copernicus believed in another theory known as the **geocentric theory**. This theory held that the Earth was the center of the solar system and that it neither rotated on an axis nor revolved about the Sun. In this theory everything moved about a central, stationary Earth. The daily east to west motion of celestial objects was thought, for example, to be caused by an actual rotation of the sky.

When we observe celestial objects from the Earth, motions seem more complex than they really are because they are a combination of the object's motion and the Earth's rotation and revolution. In reality it is the west to east rotation of the Earth that makes the sky appear to move from east to west. The apparent daily motion is called **diurnal motion**. Diurnal motion is comparable to the apparent westward motion of the landscape when you are riding in a car going east.

Similarly, the Earth's west to east revolution around the Sun makes the Sun appear to move eastward relative to the stars. Each day the Sun moves about one degree eastward and every month it enters a new constellation. In one year the Sun makes a complete circuit through the twelve constellations known as the **zodiacal constellations**. The Sun's apparent yearly path is called the **ecliptic.**

Because planets orbit the Sun in the same direction and in about the same plane as the Earth, they also seem to move eastward through the zodiacal constellations, and as they move they are never very far from the ecliptic. The planets, however, do not circle the ecliptic in one year. The time it takes a planet to move around the ecliptic depends on the planet's period of revolution and hence on its distance from the Sun. The combined motions of a planet and the Earth sometimes makes a planet reverse its eastward motion and seem to move westward. This "backing up" is called **retrograde** motion. For planets farther from the Sun than the Earth, retrograde motion occurs when the faster moving Earth overtakes and passes the slower moving planet. You may have observed a similar phenomenon if you have ever sped by a slower moving car and looked back at the car you passed in your rear view mirror!

The Moon's monthly revolution around the Earth also causes it to appear to move eastward around the ecliptic. But since the Moon revolves around the Earth in about one month it circles the ecliptic every month. The Moon's motion is very rapid compared to that of the Sun and planets. Every day it travels some twelve degrees farther to the east and as it moves through the zodiacal constellations we see it going through phases.

Viewed from the Earth the motions of celestial objects seem exceedingly complex and it is easy to understand why it required centuries to sort out and explain these motions.

CHAPTER 2

Locating Objects on the Earth and in the Sky

THE GEOGRAPHICAL SYSTEM OF COORDINATES

Latitude and longitude are the coordinates used to locate a place on the Earth's surface. **Latitude** is the number of degrees that a place is north or south of the equator. For example, a city on the equator has a latitude of 0 degrees, the north pole has a latitude of 90 degrees north, and a point midway between the north pole and the equator has a latitude of 45 degrees north. **Longitude** is the number of degrees that a place is east or west of Greenwich, England. The longitude of a city is always between 0 and 180 degrees west or 0 and 180 degrees east. Greenwich has a latitude of 52 degrees north and a longitude of 0 degrees. Detroit, Michigan has a latitude of 42 degrees north and a longitude of about 83 degrees west.

Longitudes are sometimes expressed in units of time rather than in angular units. The connection between time and angle comes from the fact that the Earth rotates through 360 degrees in 24 hours or through 15 degrees in 1 hour. Thus, 1 hour is equivalent to 15 degrees. Likewise, in 1 minute the Earth turns through 15 minutes of arc, and in 1 second of time it turns through 15 seconds of arc. Since the terms second and minute can refer to both time and angular measurement, notice that the phrase "of arc" is used to indicate angular units. Recall that there are 360 degrees in a circle, 60 minutes of arc in 1 degree, and 60 seconds of arc in 1 minute of arc.

Since 15 degrees is equivalent to 1 hour, 90 degrees is equivalent to 6 hours, 180 degrees is equivalent to 12 hours, etc. Expressed in time units the longitude of Greenwich, England is 0 hours 0 minutes and that of Detroit, Michigan is 5 hours 35 minutes west of Greenwich.

THE CELESTIAL SPHERE

If you go out on a clear evening and look up at the sky it seems as though you are at the center of a large inverted bowl that comes down and meets the earth in a big circle. This circle is called the **astronomical horizon.** Actually, you can only see this if you are out on the sea or a large plain. Usually the astronomical horizon is hidden by trees and buildings, and what is seen is the **visible horizon.** Many years ago Greek astronomers imagined that there was another part to the sky below the astronomical horizon. The entire sky, they suggested, was a sphere with half of the sphere hidden by the Earth. Today, the sky sphere is often called the **celestial sphere.**

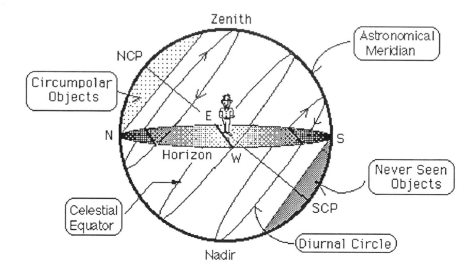

Figure 2.1 The Celestial Sphere

Figure 2.1 shows the celestial sphere. Notice that you, the observer, are at the center of the sphere and that the astronomical horizon divides the sphere into two equal parts. The point directly overhead is called the **zenith** and the point directly underfoot is known as the **nadir.** Around the horizon are the four **cardinal points**; North, East, South, and West.

Because the Earth rotates from west to east, all celestial objects seem to move in the opposite direction, from east to west. Objects rise on the eastern horizon and set on the western horizon. The paths that objects trace out in one day are known as **diurnal circles** and also as **declination circles.** A few of these circles are shown in Figure 2.1.

Notice that these circles make an angle with the horizon but they are all parallel to one another.

The diurnal circle that passes through the east and west points is called the **celestial equator**. The angle that it makes with the horizon is always equal to 90 degrees minus the observer's latitude (see Figure 2.3). All objects seem to rotate about an imaginary axis passing through the observer and two points in the sky called the **north celestial pole (NCP)** and the **south celestial pole (SCP)**.

The NCP lies directly above the north point on the horizon. The North Star, **Polaris**, is very close to the NCP. Polaris is the last star in the handle of Ursa Minor, better known as the Little Dipper. The NCP's angular distance above the north point is always equal to the observer's latitude. For example, at latitude 45 degrees north the NCP is 45 degrees above the north point, while at latitude 90 degrees north, Polaris is 90 degrees from the horizon at the zenith.

THE DAILY MOTION OF CELESTIAL OBJECTS

An observer's **astronomical meridian** is the circle that passes through the south point on the horizon, the zenith, the NCP, the north point on the horizon, and the nadir. This circle divides the sky into an eastern and a western half. When an object is rising it is to the east of the meridian and when it is setting it is to the west of the meridian. The part of the meridian above the horizon is called the **upper meridian** and that below the horizon is known as the **lower meridian**.

When an object crosses the upper meridian and is at its greatest distance above the horizon it is said to be at **upper transit**. At **lower transit** an object usually lies below the horizon on the lower meridian. Objects are at upper and lower transit once each day.

Some objects rise directly at the east point, while others rise north or south of east. It is important to realize that objects which rise at the east point must set at the west point. Likewise objects that rise in the north-east must set in the north-west and objects that rise in the south-east must set in the south-west. In addition, some objects remain below the horizon and are never seen, while some remain above the horizon and are always visible. Objects that always stay above the horizon are called **circumpolar objects** since they circle around the Pole Star Polaris.

The time that an object spends above the horizon depends, essentially, on where it rises. Objects that rise at the east point are above the horizon for twelve hours and below it for twelve hours. Objects that rise in the north-east remain above the horizon for more than twelve hours and those that rise in the south-east are above the horizon for less than twelve hours.

Any given star always rises and sets at the same point on the horizon and hence is above the horizon for the same amount of time every day of the year. This is not true, however, for the Sun, Moon, and planets. In the summer in the northern hemisphere the Sun rises in the northeast and days are long, while during the winter the Sun rises in the southeast and days are short. Twice a year, on the **vernal equinox** (March 21) and the **autumnal equinox** (September 21), the Sun rises at the east point and is above the horizon twelve hours and below it for twelve hours. The longest day of the year occurs on the **summer solstice** (June 21) and the shortest on the **winter solstice** (December 21).

THE HORIZON SYSTEM OF COORDINATES

Longitude and latitude locate a place on the surface of the spherical Earth. Similar coordinates are used to locate objects in the sky. One such set of coordinates is called the **horizon system**. The coordinates in this system are termed altitude and azimuth (see Figure 2.2).

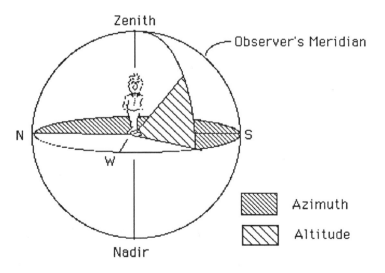

Figure 2.2   The Horizon System

Altitude is the angular distance that an object is above the horizon. Altitude ranges from 0 to +90 degrees for objects on or above the horizon and from 0 to -90 degrees for objects below the horizon.

Azimuth is the angular distance measured from the north point, eastward around the horizon to the object. This coordinate ranges from 0 to 360 degrees.

The following table lists some altitudes and azimuths. The nn for the zenith's azimuth indicates that azimuth is not needed since the zenith is the only point with an altitude of 90 degrees.

Object	Altitude (deg)	Azimuth (deg)
N	0	0
E	0	90
S	0	180
W	0	270
Zenith	90	nn
NCP	lat	0
Star rise	0	0 to 180
Star set	0	180 to 360
Upper transit	max	0 or 180

The coordinates of the cardinal points, the NCP, and the zenith are always the same, but this is definitely not true for celestial objects. An object's altitude and azimuth change continually as it moves from east to west. When an object is rising its altitude is 0 and its azimuth is a minimum value somewhere between 0 and 180 degrees. When it is setting its altitude is again 0 degrees but its azimuth lies somewhere between 180 and 360 degrees. An object is said to be at upper transit when it has its maximum possible altitude. This usually occurs when the object lies directly above the south point and thus has an azimuth of 180 degrees. However, circumpolar objects have an azimuth of 0 degrees when they are at either upper or lower transit.

Figure 2.3 is drawn with the Earth at the center of the celestial sphere. An observer is shown on the Earth in the northern hemisphere at midlatitude, halfway between the equator and the north (NP) and south (SP) poles. The angle between the observer and the equator is the observer's latitude (about 40 degrees in this example). As always, the point over the observer's head is the zenith and the point underfoot is the nadir. The horizon is drawn as a line tangent to the Earth and also as a circle dividing the sky into two hemispheres.

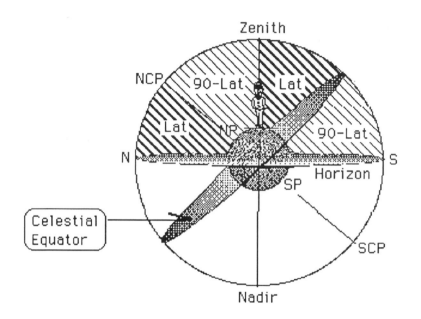

Figure 2.3   The Celestial Equator and Poles

In the figure the Earth's axis of rotation has been extended out to the sky and intersects it at the north (NCP) and south (SCP) celestial poles. Likewise, extending the Earth's equator produces the circle called the celestial equator. Thus, the celestial poles and equator are simply the astronomical counterparts of the Earth's poles and equator. Notice that the celestial equator divides the sky into a northern and southern hemisphere. The celestial poles are located 90 degrees north and south of the celestial equator.

The size of the Earth is really insignificant compared to the distance to even the closest stars. If the Earth in the figure were drawn on the same scale as the sky it would be but a point, the observer would be at the center, and the figure would look like Figure 2.2. In other words you, the observer, always seem to be at the center of things because of the Earth's smallness.

Now try to imagine yourself in Figure 2.3 standing at the Earth's north pole, latitude 90 degrees. The NCP pole would be at your zenith with a 90 degree altitude, and the celestial equator and horizon would coincide. Next picture yourself on the Earth's equator at 0 degrees latitude. Here the celestial equator would pass through the zenith and the NCP would lie at the north point on the horizon and have an altitude of 0 degrees. Finally if you were alongside the observer at latitude 40 degrees north the NCP would be at an altitude of 45 degrees above the north point on the horizon. From these observations you can conclude that in general,

The altitude of the NCP is always numerically equal to the latitude of the observer.

One of the potential disadvantages of the horizon system is that diurnal motion causes altitude and azimuth to change with time. Another is that the coordinates depend on an observer's latitude. This is because observers at different latitudes on a spherical Earth have different zeniths and horizons (see Figure 2.4). At any instant a star above one observer's horizon need not be above the other's horizon.

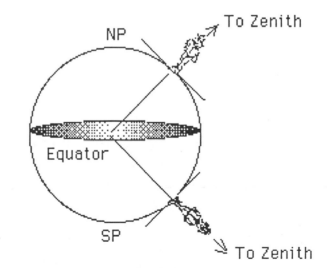

Figure 2.4   Zenith and Horizon

THE EQUATORIAL SYSTEM OF COORDINATES

The disadvantages of the horizon system are eliminated in the **equatorial system** of coordinates. While the horizon system is a local system depending on time and location, the equatorial system is more general. It can be used by any observer at any time. This system is similar to the geographical coordinate system. Latitude and longitude are independent of time because the coordinate grid is marked out on the rotating Earth and moves with it. In a similar fashion, the coordinate grid of the equatorial system is marked out on the rotating celestial sphere.

Figure 2.5 shows the celestial sphere without either the Earth or the observer in the picture.

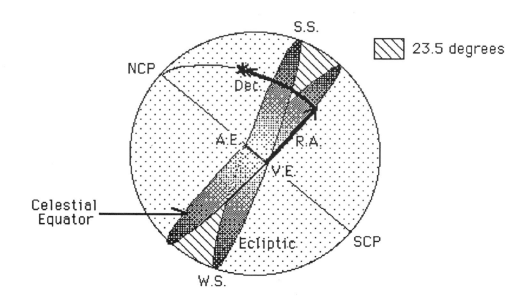

Figure 2.5   The Equatorial System of Coordinates

The Earth's revolution about the Sun makes the Sun appear to move eastward among the twelve constellations known as the **zodiacal constellations**. Each month the Sun is in a different zodiacal constellation. The circle labeled **ecliptic** represents the Sun's yearly path through the zodiacal constellations. It is actually the Earth's orbital plane extended out to the sky. The ecliptic is inclined to the celestial equator by a 23.5 degree angle because the Earth's equator is tipped 23.5 degrees relative to its orbital plane.

The Sun moves counterclockwise (eastward) along the ecliptic about one degree per day. On March 21 it is at the point marked V.E. On June 21 it is at point S.S. On September 21 the Sun is at point A.E. and on December 21 it is at point W.S. These points are called the vernal equinox, the summer solstice, the autumnal equinox, and the winter solstice, respectively.

While we often think of the the equinoxes and solstices as dates, they are also points on the ecliptic. The vernal equinox, for example, is in the zodiacal constellation of **Pisces**. These points, like celestial objects, have a diurnal motion. The vernal equinox rises at the east point and sets at the west point on the horizon every day in the year. However, the Sun is at the vernal equinox (in Pisces) only on March 21. On this date the Sun, along with the equinox, rises at the east point and sets at the west point. The daily motion of the Sun is discussed in more detail in the next section.

In Figure 2.5 a star is shown on an arc passing through the NCP. This arc is part of a circle that also passes through the SCP. Any circle that passes through the celestial poles is called an **hour circle**, and there are an infinite number of these circles. Each celestial object lies on an hour circle and is located on the celestial sphere by the coordinates of declination and right ascension.

Declination is an object's angular distance north or south of the celestial equator. It is measured along the hour circle through the object and is expressed in angular units. Declination is similar to latitude on the Earth's surface.

Right ascension is an object's angular distance from the vernal equinox. It is measured from the equinox eastward (counterclockwise) around the celestial equator to the hour circle containing the object. Right ascension is expressed in time units and is similar to longitude on the Earth's surface.

Object	Declination (degrees)	Right Ascension (Hours)	Sun Date
Vernal equinox	0.0	0	Mar 21
Summer solstice	23.5	6	Jun 21
Autumnal equinox	0.0	12	Sep 21
Winter solstice	-23.5	18	Dec 21
NCP	90.0	nn	
SCP	-90.0	nn	

The table above lists a few declinations and right ascensions. Note that objects on the celestial equator have declinations of 0 degrees, objects north of the celestial equator have positive declinations, and objects south of the celestial equator have negative declinations.

The major advantage of the equatorial system is that the coordinates of stars are essentially independent of time and the location of the observer. This is NOT true, however, for solar system objects. Each year as the Sun moves around the ecliptic its right ascension and declination vary as shown in the table. The Sun's declination ranges from plus 23.5 degrees to minus 23.5 degrees and its right ascension varies from 0 hours through 24 hours. You might think of the Sun as a person who goes north for the winter months and south during the summer months! The Moon cycles through its coordinates in about one month, while the time required for a planet's coordinates to change depends on its period of revolution.

THE DAILY MOTION OF THE SUN

Figures 2.6, 2.7, and 2.8 illustrate the daily motion of the Sun on the dates of the equinoxes and solstices as seen from latitudes 90 degrees north, 45 degrees north, and 0 degrees, respectively. In all cases the altitude of the NCP has been drawn equal to the latitude.

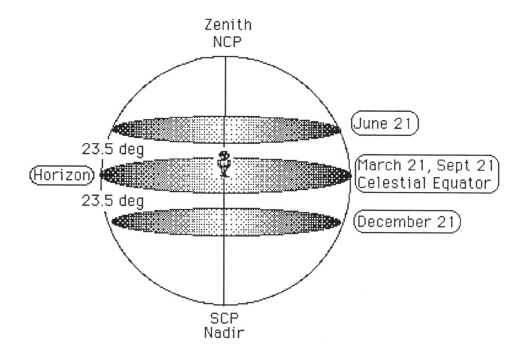

Figure 2.6   Latitude 90 degrees North

On the dates of the **equinoxes**, when the Sun's declination is 0 degrees, its daily path is the celestial equator. At the equator and at middle latitudes it rises at the east point and sets at the west point, remaining above the horizon for twelve hours and below the horizon for twelve hours. However, at the north pole where the horizon and celestial equator are one and the same circle, the Sun circles around the horizon and never sets.

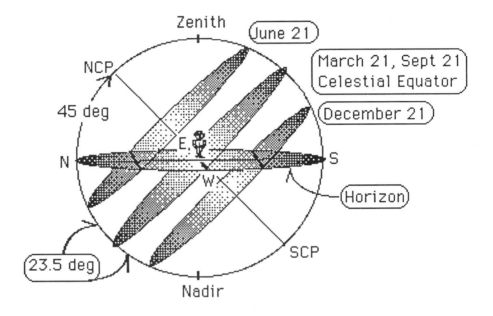

Figure 2.7   Latitude 45 degrees North

On the **summer solstice** the Sun is 23.5 degrees north of the celestial equator. At midlatitudes the Sun rises north of east, sets north of west, and is above the horizon longer than it is below the horizon. Days are longer than nights. At the north pole the Sun circles parallel to the horizon at an altitude of 23.5 degrees and never sets. Hence, daylight lasts 24 hours.

On the **winter solstice**, when the Sun's declination is -23.5 degrees, the Sun is south of the celestial equator. At midlatitudes the Sun rises south of east, sets south of west, and is below the horizon longer than it is above the horizon. Days are shorter than nights. At the north pole the Sun is 23.5 degrees below the horizon and never rises. The night is 24 hours long.

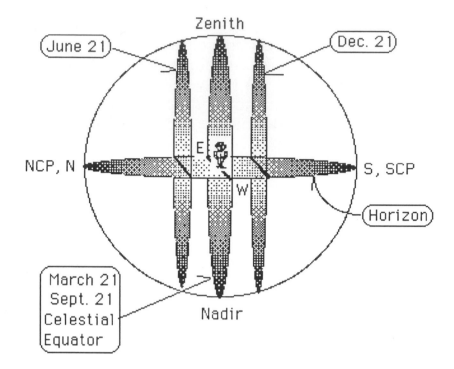

Figure 2.8 Latitude 0 degrees, the Equator

At the Earth's poles and equator there are some interesting variations on the theme of night and day. For example, at the north pole, between March 21 and September 21, when the Sun's declination is positive, the Sun is always above the horizon. But between September 21 and March 21, when the Sun's declination is negative, it is always below the horizon. However, at the equator the Sun is above the horizon twelve hours and below the horizon twelve hours every day of the year. Also, the equator is the only place where the Sun is at the zenith at noon on the dates of the equinoxes.

At the equator, not only the Sun, but all celestial objects rise and set vertically to the horizon. This means that each day every object is above the horizon for twelve hours and below it for twelve hours and there are no circumpolar objects. However, at the north pole, where the horizon and celestial equator are one and the same circle, any object having a negative declination lies below the horizon and any object with a positive declination is above the horizon. Since daily paths are parallel to the horizon, stars with positive declinations always remain above the horizon (circumpolar) and stars with negative declinations are never seen!

SUMMARY

The coordinate systems discussed above are summarized in the following table using the general terminology of spherical coordinate systems.

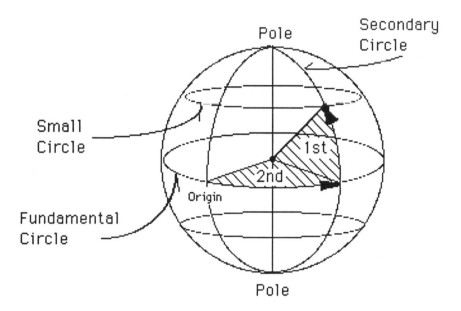

Figure 2.9   Spherical Coordinate Systems

DEFINITIONS

Great circle: The intersection between a sphere and a plane passing through the center of the sphere.

Small circle: The intersection between a sphere and a plane not passing through the center of the sphere.

Fundamental circle: A great circle chosen as a reference circle.

Poles: The two points 90 degrees in either direction from the fundamental circle.

Secondary circle: Any great circle through the poles of a sphere.

Origin: A chosen point on the fundamental circle.

First coordinate: The angular distance above or below the fundamental circle measured along the secondary circle through the object.

Second coordinate: The angular distance measured from the origin in a specified direction along the fundamental circle to the secondary circle through the object.

SUMMARY

Spherical Coordinate Systems

General	Geographic	Horizon	Equatorial
Fundamental circle	Earth's equator	Horizon	Celestial equator
Poles	North and South Poles	Zenith and Nadir	NCP & SCP
Secondary circles	Meridians of Longitude	Vertical Circle	Hour circles
Origin	Greenwich, England	North Point	Vernal equinox
First coordinate	Latitude	Altitude	Declination
Second coordinate	Longitude	Azimuth	Right ascension

CHAPTER 3

Telling Time by the Stars

INTRODUCTION

Sunrise, sunset, the sequence of day and night, the cycle of lunar phases, the changing seasons, all mark the passage of time. In the beginning, timekeeping involved merely counting the days, months, and years. But at some time in the distant past people began to count the hours. One of the earliest methods used observations of shadows. When the Sun rises in the east shadows are long and point westward but as the Sun's altitude increases shadows shorten and swing northward. At noon shadows are at their shortest and point directly north. Then through the afternoon they lengthen once again, stretching eastward away from the setting Sun. The hour of the day can be reckoned by either the direction or length of the shadows.

In the opening lines of the "Parson's Prologue" Chaucer writes

> It was four o'clock according to my guess,
> Since eleven feet, a little more or less,
> My shadow at the time did fall,
> Considering that I myself am six feet tall

And in his "Man of Law's Tale" he notes

> ...the shadow of each tree
> Had reached a length of that same quantity
> As was the body which had cast the shade
> And on this basis he conclusion made:
> ...for that day, and in that latitude,
> The time was ten o'clock...

When it was realized that the directions of shadows were more accurate indications of time, the sundial became the preferred device for recording the time of day. One early fragment of a sundial dates from about 1500 B.C., and around 600 B.C. the Greek philosopher Anaximander is thought to have introduced the sundial into Greece. By 200 B.C. sundials were very common in Rome, and a contemporary of Julius Caesar listed more than a dozen different types of dials. The first sundials were probably sticks stuck vertically in the ground. But perhaps by the first century A.D. it was discovered that the shadow of a slanting object, parallel to the Earth's axis, was a more accurate timeteller than the shadow of a vertical one. The "modern" sundial had been invented and it measured the passage of time for centuries.

Today accurate atomic clocks measure time and even inexpensive watches do a very good job. But clocks of whatever kind must initially be set to the correct time, and this is still done by observing the motions of the Sun, Moon, and stars.

DEFINING TIME

The time told by a sundial is called local apparent time but there are, in fact, many other types of time, including local mean time, local sidereal time, standard time, and daylight saving time. Different types of time can be defined by choosing specific celestial objects to mark the passage of time.

The Sun is one obvious choice, but in principle one could use the Moon, as some early civilizations did, or even the planets. However, the most frequently chosen objects are the real **Sun**, the **Vernal Equinox**, and something called the **Mean Sun**, which is a fictitious Sun that moves along the celestial equator with the real Sun's average (mean) speed. These objects are used, respectively, to define local apparent time, local sidereal time, and local mean time.

But by whatever name, there are always 24 hours in a day. To avoid the sometimes confusing A.M. and P.M. designations a 24 hour clock is often used. A day always begins at 0, or 24, hours. On this system, 6 A.M. is 6 hours, noon is 12 hours, and 6 P.M. is 18 hours. Technically speaking,

> **one day** is the time interval between two similar meridian crossings of the chosen celestial object.

An observer's **astronomical meridian** (see Figure 3.1) is the circle that passes through the south point on the horizon, the zenith, the

NCP, the north point on the horizon, and the nadir. This circle divides the sky into an eastern and a western half. When an object is rising it is to the east of the meridian and when it is setting it is to the west of the meridian. The meridian above the horizon is called the **upper meridian** and that below the horizon, the **lower meridian**.

When an object crosses the upper meridian and has its greatest altitude it is said to be at **upper transit**. At **lower transit** an object has its smallest altitude and usually lies below the horizon on the lower meridian. Objects are at upper and lower transit once each day.

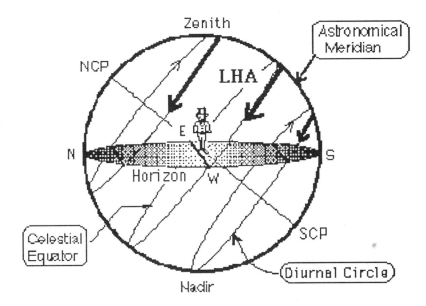

Figure 3.1   The Astronomical Meridian

A **local apparent day** is the time interval between two lower transits of the real Sun. Likewise, a **local mean day** is the time interval between two lower transits of the Mean Sun. Both types of days begin when the respective suns are below the horizon at lower transit. On the other hand, the **local sidereal day** is the time between two upper transits of the vernal equinox, which means a sidereal day starts when the vernal equinox is above the horizon.

At any instant, local time depends on the chosen object's position relative to the observer's astronomical meridian. This position is given by the **local hour angle (LHA)**, which is simply the number of hours that have passed since an object was at upper transit. At upper transit an object's LHA is 0 hours while at lower transit it is 12 hours. In other words, the LHA indicates how far an object is to the west of an observer's meridian. An object 6 hours to the west of the astronomical meridian has an LHA of 6 hours and an object 6 hours to the east has an LHA of 18 hours. An object to the east is sometimes said to have a negative LHA. That is, 18 hours is equivalent to a minus (-) 6 hours.

The Sun's LHA is used to define **local apparent time (LAT)**. At noon, when the Sun is at upper transit, its LHA is 0 hours and the LAT is 12 hours. One hour later its LHA will be 1 hour and the LAT will be 13 hours. In general, the local apparent time is equal to the LHA of the Sun plus 12 hours:

$$\text{LAT} = \text{LHA}_{\text{Sun}} + 12 \text{ hours}$$

Notice that 12 hours must be added to the Sun's LHA because the local apparent day begins when the Sun is at lower transit. Formulae like the one above sometimes yield values greater than 24 hours. In such cases one must subtract 24 from the value. As has been mentioned, local apparent time is the type of time told by a sundial.

The definition of **local mean time (LMT)** is similar to that of LAT except that the LHA of the Mean Sun is used. Thus,

$$\text{LMT} = \text{LHA}_{\text{Mean Sun}} + 12 \text{ hours}$$

Local sidereal time (LST) is defined as the LHA of the vernal equinox (VE), that is,

$$\text{LST} = \text{LHA}_{\text{VE}}$$

Notice that it is not necessary to add 12 hours to the LHA of the vernal equinox because the sidereal day begins when the vernal equinox is at upper transit. At this time its LHA is zero and the LST is also zero. This is the beginning of the local sidereal day.

LOCATING THE VERNAL EQUINOX

Because sidereal time is defined as the hour angle of the vernal equinox, LST indicates how far the vernal equinox is to the west of the astronomical meridian. For example, if the LST is 0 hours the vernal equinox is on the meridian and if LST is 6 hours the vernal equinox is just setting at the west point. Also, at a LST of 12 hours the vernal equinox is at lower transit and at 18 hours it is rising at the east point on the horizon.

It can be shown from the definitions of right ascension and local sidereal time that the LST is equal to the right ascension of any object at upper transit, that is,

$$LST = R.A._{upper\ transit}$$

In other words, the LST indicates what objects are on the meridian. For example, all objects having a right ascension of 0 hours are at upper transit at an LST of 0 hours and at an LST of 14 hours all objects with that right ascension are at upper transit.

A more general relationship states that the local sidereal time is equal to the right ascension of any object plus that object's local hour angle:

$$LST = R.A. + LHA$$

For example, if a star having an R.A. of 3 hours is 2 hours west of the meridian, then the LST must be 5 hours. The formula can also be used to find the LHA of any object if the LST and the object's R.A. are known. Solving for LHA gives,

$$LHA = LST - R.A.$$

COMPARING TIMES

Since the Earth moves 360 degrees around the Sun in approximately 360 days, it must move about 1 degree along its orbit each day. Because of this the Sun appears to move eastward along the ecliptic by 1 degree per day (see Figure 3.2). Actually both the Earth and the Sun move a little less than 1 degree per day because there are 365 1/4 days in a year rather than 360 days. As viewed from the Earth, the constellations out in the Sun's direction are above the horizon during the day. But as the Sun moves eastward relative to these stars they rise earlier and earlier and eventually become visible at night. This results in different constellations being visible during different times of the year.

In time units, 1 degree is equivalent to 4 minutes of time. Thus, the Sun's eastward motion relative to the stars causes the stars to rise 4 minutes earlier each day. A star that rises with the Sun today will rise 4 minutes before the Sun tomorrow and 8 minutes earlier than the Sun the next day. Likewise, a star that rises at 9 P.M. tonight will rise at 8:56 tomorrow and at 8:52 the next night.

A sidereal clock runs at a different rate than clocks keeping LAT or LMT. In fact, compared to these clocks, a sidereal clock gains approximately 4 minutes each day. The reason for this gain is the same reason that stars rise about 4 minutes earlier each day.

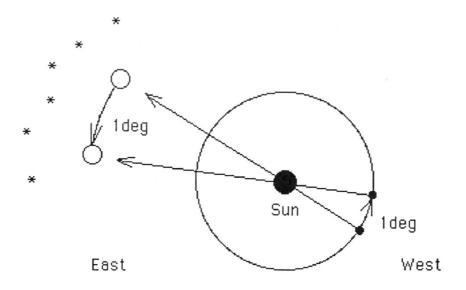

Figure 3.2   The Sun's Eastward Motion

If a sidereal clock gains about 4 minutes each day compared to, say, an LAT clock, in 30 days it will gain 2 hours, and in 1 year it will gain 24 hours or 1 full day. It follows that there are 366 sidereal days in 365 solar days and that the length of a sidereal day is 365/366 the length of a solar day. This fraction implies that a sidereal day is 3 min 56 sec shorter than a solar day. This is the actual daily gain of a sidereal clock over other clocks. Also, stars actually rise 3 min 56 sec earlier each day, rather than 4 minutes.

A sidereal clock's full day gain in 1 year implies that once each year a sidereal clock must tell the same time as the other types of clocks. In fact LAT and LST are the same at about midnight on the date of the autumnal equinox. But each day thereafter the faster sidereal clock gains 3 min 56 sec.

Many centuries ago it was discovered that the Sun does not move uniformly along the ecliptic. This nonuniform motion is partly due to the fact that the Earth's orbital speed changes (Kepler's second law). The Earth moves fastest in the winter when it is closest to the Sun and slowest in the summer when it is farthest from the Sun. As the Earth's orbital speed changes so does the apparent eastward motion of the Sun. Another reason for the nonuniformity is the 23.5 degree inclination of the Earth's rotational axis to the orbital plane.

The nonuniform motion of the Sun causes local apparent time to be nonuniform. For example, on days when the Sun moves more than one degree eastward the time between lower transits is greater than usual and the day is longer. The reverse is the case on days when the Sun moves less than one degree. So local apparent days are not always the same length. If there is one thing that we insist on today, it is that every day be the same length. The Mean Sun was invented to eliminate this problem. The Mean Sun moves eastward along the celestial equator, rather than along the ecliptic, and it moves with the real Sun's average (mean) speed. Thus, the Mean Sun moves uniformly and this, in turn, insures that local mean time is also uniform.

It is interesting to note that the actual Sun would move uniformly if the Earth's axis of rotation were perpendicular to its orbital plane and if the Earth revolved about the Sun in a circular orbit. If this were the case the real Sun would move uniformly eastward along the celestial equator and would always rise at the east point on the horizon and set at the west point. The Sun would always spend 12 hours above the horizon and 12 hours below the horizon, and seasons as we know them would not exist.

THE EQUATION OF TIME

Local apparent and local mean times are related by the **equation of time** (E), which is defined as the difference between local apparent time and local mean time:

$$E = LAT - LMT$$

During the year, because of its nonuniform motion, the actual Sun is sometimes ahead of and sometimes behind the Mean Sun. The equation of time can be either positive or negative. When LAT is greater than LMT, E is positive. When LAT is less than LMT, E is negative. The equation of time ranges between about plus and minus 16 minutes. The values of E can be computed, and repeat themselves each year (see Table 3.1).

Table 3.1 The Equation of Time

Date		E	Date		E
Jan	01	-3.5	July	10	- 5.0
	11	-7.9		20	- 6.1
	21	-11.3		30	- 6.2
	31	-13.6			
			Aug	09	- 5.4
Feb	10	-14.4		19	- 3.6
	20	-14.0		29	- 0.9
Mar	02	-12.4	Sept	08	+2.3
	12	-10.0		18	+5.8
	22	-7.1		28	+9.2
Apr	01	-4.1	Oct	08	+12.3
	11	-1.2		18	+14.7
	21	+1.2		28	+16.1
May	01	+2.9	Nov	07	+16.2
	11	+3.7		17	+15.0
	21	+3.6		27	+12.4
	31	+2.6			
			Dec	07	+8.5
June	10	+0.9		17	+3.9
	20	-1.2		27	- 1.0
	30	-3.3			

From the preceding definition of E it follows that

$$LMT = LAT - E$$

This equation can be used to calculate LMT if LAT and E are known. Likewise, it is possible to find LAT knowing LMT and E, since

$$LAT = LMT + E$$

STANDARD TIME

The times discussed so far have been local times defined in terms of an object's local hour angle. They are unique to a particular observer because hour angle is measured from an observer's meridian and observers at different longitudes have different meridians. For example, when the Sun is at upper transit on a particular observer's astronomical meridian its LHA is 0 hours and the LAT is 12 noon. But for an observer 1 hour to the west in longitude, the Sun would be 1 hour from upper transit, to the east of this observer's meridian, and the LAT would be 11 A.M. The difference between the local times of two observers is exactly equal to the difference in their longitudes:

difference in longitude = difference in local time

Since the local time to the west of any particular observer is earlier by an amount equal to the longitude difference, the time to the west (LT_{west}) is found by subtracting the longitude difference from the observer's local time (LT_{obs}),

$$LT_{west} = LT_{obs} - \text{longitude difference}$$

However, the longitude difference is added to find the time to the east:

$$LT_{east} = LT_{obs} + \text{longitude difference}$$

In the above equations the local time (LT) can be LAT, LMT, or LST.

Longitude is measured east and west of the **Prime Meridian** passing through **Greenwich**, England. Since the continental United States lies to the west of Greenwich, the time everywhere in the U.S. is earlier than that at Greenwich, while at points to the east of Greenwich the time is later.

Nowadays it is obviously impractical for everyone to keep their own local time. The world is divided into a number of **standard time zones**, each covering 1 hour (15 degrees) of longitude. The meridian passing through the center of each zone is called the **standard time meridian**. In the U.S. the longitudes of the standard time meridians are 5 hours west, 6 hours west, 7 hours west, and 8 hours west. The corresponding time zones are Eastern Standard, Central Standard, Mountain Standard, and Pacific Standard. The times kept in these zones are called Eastern Standard Time **(EST)**, Central Standard Time **(CST)**, Mountain Standard Time (MST), and Pacific Standard Time **(PST)**, respectively.

Standard time is defined as the local mean time of the standard time meridian. Within each zone everyone agrees to keep the LMT of the zone's standard time meridian. For example, in the EST zone each watch is set to read the LMT of an observer at 5 hours west longitude.

Since the zones are 1 hour wide there are 30 minutes (7.5 degrees) on either side of the central meridian. Within each zone some people will be located to the west of the standard meridian and some people to the east. The LMT of an individual living at the western edge of the zone is 30 minutes earlier than the standard time, while at the eastern edge of the zone the LMT is 30 minutes later. Because of this, standard times do not usually agree with an observer's LMT. In addition, the LAT differs from the LMT by the equation of time. The net result is that LAT may differ from standard time by as much as 46 minutes. Put somewhat differently, a watch keeping standard time is not a good indicator of the Sun's hour angle or position in the sky.

During the spring and summer months most states go on **daylight saving time (DST)**. This is simply accomplished by setting clocks ahead 1 hour; in other words,

daylight saving time = standard time + 1 hour

In the autumn, clocks are set back by 1 hour to return to standard time. Daylight saving time essentially takes 1 hour off the beginning of the day and adds it to the end of the day.

Astronomical events and the positions of celestial objects are often given for the LMT at Greenwich, England. The **Greenwich Mean Time (GMT)** is sometimes referred to as **Universal Time (UT)**. A universal time can be converted into a standard time by subtracting (if you are west) or adding (if you are east) the longitude of your standard time meridian. For example, a Universal Time of 10 hours corresponds to an EST of 5 hours and a CST of 4 hours.

Chapter 4

The Voyager Program and Coordinate Systems

Project 1 Getting Around in Voyager

An Introduction to Voyager

Project 2 Looking Around the Horizon

The Horizon System

Project 3 Cruising the Zodiac

Locating Constellations and Planets

Project 4 Tracking the Sun, Moon, and Planets

The Equatorial System

PROJECT 1

Getting Around in Voyager

GOAL: TO BECOME FAMILIAR WITH THE VOYAGER PROGRAM

UP AND RUNNING

There are numerous ways of starting the Voyager program, depending on whether your Macintosh has one or two floppy disk drives, a hard disk drive, or if it is part of a local area network. You should consult your Voyager manual or your instructor for the best way to get the program up and running in your own particular setting.

No matter what the setting, every Mac has a pointing device called a **mouse**. By moving the mouse with your hand you can move a pointer called a **cursor** anywhere on the monitor screen. Clicking the mouse button either once or twice causes things to happen. What happens usually depends on the number of clicks and what the cursor is positioned on. Rapidly clicking twice when the cursor is on the small picture of the **Voyager Observatory** will start the program. Sometimes you may have to hold the button down while you move the mouse. This is called **dragging** the mouse.

Voyager is a very friendly and forgiving program so you can point, click, and drag all you wish without any fear of hurting anything. In fact, you can learn a great deal by just mousing around.

THE START UP SCREEN

The first thing you will see on your monitor when Voyager is up and running is the **start up** screen. The specific times, date, and objects displayed may be different but the general screen layout should be the same as shown in Figure 1.1. The top portion of the start up screen is called the **menu bar**. Each word in this bar (File, Edit, Control, Field, Display, Options) is a **menu** consisting of a list of **commands** (see Appendix 1).

You can **Open** a menu by positioning the cursor over a word in the menu bar. While pressing the mouse button, move the mouse downward. As you drag the mouse, an item list appears and each item is highlighted with a black bar as the cursor moves over it. If an item is a command, such as **Quit** in the **File** menu, releasing the mouse button with the item highlighted executes the command. The **Quit** command lets you exit from the Voyager program. An item that is lighter than the other items in a menu is inactive and can not be used until Voyager decides it is appropriate to do so.

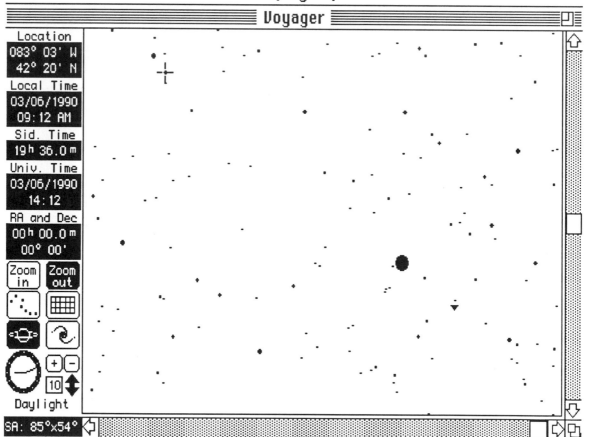

Figure 1.1 **The Voyager Start Up Screen**

If there is a black arrowhead next to an item, you should keep the mouse button depressed and move the cursor towards the arrow. This opens up a **submenu** containing another list of items. Releasing the mouse button with an item highlighted will, as before, execute the command.

Some items have a series of three dots (...) next to them. Releasing the button on these dotted items causes a **dialog** box to appear on the screen (see Figure 1.3). Dialog boxes are used to enter information that the program requires.

A number of items have a symbol and a letter next to them. The symbol is the same one that is printed on the keyboard **command** key, immediately to the left of the space bar. By holding down the Command key and pressing the letter you can execute the command at any time without using the mouse.

On the left side of the start up screen there are a number of boxes that display useful information. The **Location** box displays longitude and latitude. Date and watch time are shown in the **Local Time** box. The local sidereal time is displayed in the **Sidereal Time** box and the time at Greenwich is indicated in the **Universal Time** box. The box labeled **RA and Dec** shows the coordinates of the center of the screen. Each of the boxes is updated to reflect any changes that are made in time, date, or location.

The smaller boxes are command boxes. Clicking the mouse button when the cursor is over any of these boxes tells Voyager to do such things as put a coordinate grid on the screen or draw constellation lines.

Project Result 1: Try clicking on each of the small boxes and record what happens in the project report form.

Scroll bars are located on the right and bottom of the screen. With these bars you can move the region of the sky being viewed up and down as well as left and right. You might think of looking at the sky through a window frame. As the frame is moved, you view different areas of the sky. Try clicking on the arrows at either end of the scroll bars. Next drag the white box in each scroll bar to see what happens. Finally, try clicking on either side of the white scroll bar boxes.

SETTING LATITUDE AND LONGITUDE

When Voyager starts, it automatically sets your location to a predetermined latitude and longitude. You will usually want to change these values to correspond to your own latitude and longitude. To set your observing location open the **Control** menu as described above. When **Set Location** is highlighted, position the cursor over **Major Cities** and release the mouse button. The **Select City** window will appear (see Figure 1.2).

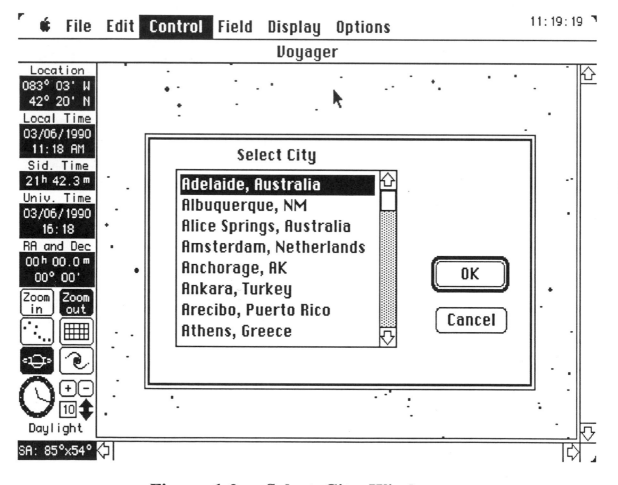

Figure 1.2   Select City Window

Drag the white scroll bar square or click on the scroll arrows until you find a **city** from which you want to observe. Release the mouse button and either **double click** on the highlighted city, click on the **OK** box, or press the Return key. You have just told the computer that you want to observe from this city. Clicking on the **Cancel** box returns you to the start up screen without changing the original location.

The above instructions might be abbreviated as

❑   **Control@Set Location@Major Cities**
❑   **Select City@City**
❑   **Double Click or OK or Return**

Another way of setting your observing location is to open the **Control** menu, highlight **Set Location**, and release the mouse button over **World Map**. Dragging the cursor within the world map continuously updates the displayed latitude and longitude to the cursor's location on the map. Releasing the button sets the location. You can also enter latitude and longitude in the designated boxes of the **World Map** dialog box.

SETTING THE TIME OF OBSERVATION

When Voyager is loaded into the Mac it reads the **system clock** and displays the present time and date in the **Local Time** box. However, you may want to view the sky at some other time or date. To do this, open the **Control** menu, drag to **Set Time**, and release the mouse button when **Local Mean Time** is highlighted. When the dialog box (Figure 1.3) appears type the year, month, and day in the appropriate boxes, using the **tab** key to go between boxes.

Instead of using the tab key you can also position the cursor in any box, click, and then type the required information. Click one of the two circles to choose **AM** or **PM** and also choose **Yes** or **No** to indicate if the time is a **daylight saving time**. When the boxes and circles have all been filled either press the Return key or click on the **OK** box to send this information to the computer. You can change any of the information in the boxes before you press the Return key by positioning the cursor in a box and pressing the **Delete** key.

These instructions might be abbreviated as

❑   **Control@Set Time@Local Mean Time**
❑   **Dialog**
❑   **OK or Return**

IMPORTANT: YOU MUST ALWAYS ENTER YOUR LATITUDE AND LONGITUDE BEFORE ENTERING THE OBSERVING TIME BECAUSE CHANGING YOUR LOCATION WILL ALSO CHANGE ANY TIME THAT YOU MAY HAVE ENTERED

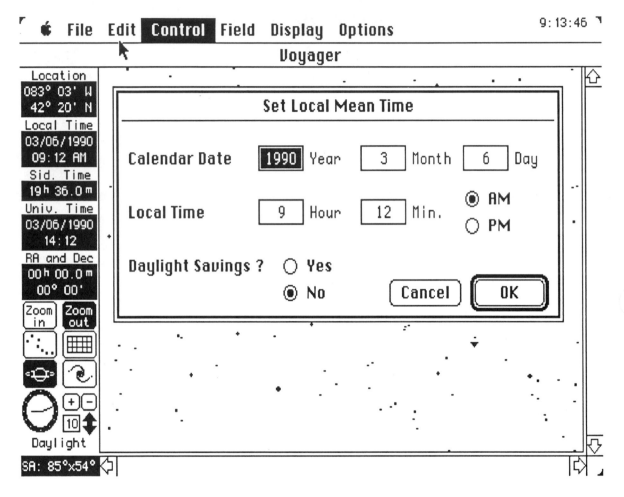

Figure 1.3 Set Local Mean Time Dialog Box

GETTING INFORMATION

At the heart of the Voyager program is a celestial database of 14,000 objects, including 9,100 stars, 3,000 deep sky objects such as galaxies and nebulae, 1,600 binary stars, 160 variable stars, the Sun, Moon, and planets. A click of the mouse button identifies any of these objects and provides information about them such as distance, temperature, size, rising and setting times, and brightness.

Project Result 2: Try clicking the mouse button when the cursor is positioned on a **star** and record the information in the project report form. Close the star's information box by clicking anywhere in the box. If an object is not visible on the screen you can usually locate it by using one of the first ten commands under the **Field** menu. Locate the **Sun** and **Mars** and record the information in the project report form.

CHANGING SKY VIEWS

With Voyager you can view the sky at any time from any place on the Earth's surface. You can also view the sky in a number of different ways by using the commands listed in the **Sky View** menu. Any view visible on the monitor screen can be printed by choosing **Print Sky Chart** in the **File** menu. Experiment with each of the views and note how they differ. Try using the scroll bars to see what happens.

Project Result 3: Choose a city close to where you were born and enter the date and time of your birth. Center on the Sun and make a printout of the sky views called **Star Atlas**, **Celestial Sphere**, **Local Horizon**, and **Planetarium**. On the printouts identify any **planets** that are in the vicinity of the **Sun**. Hand in these printouts with your project report.

IMPORTANT: BEFORE YOU PRINT A STAR CHART ALWAYS MAKE THE BLACK SKY WHITE (SEE FIGURE 1.1). TO DO THIS SELECT **WHITE SKY** IN THE **DISPLAY** MENU. DOING THIS SAVES PRINTER RIBBON!

Project Result 4: Repeat Project Result 3 for your birthday this year and note any differences you observe in the positions of the planets and Sun. Explain any differences.

Within any view screen you can zoom in for a closer look. Try holding down the mouse button and dragging the cursor to define a square on the screen. Release the button and see what happens. Once you have zoomed in using this method or by clicking the small **Zoom in** box, you can click the **Zoom out** box to get back to where you started.

MOUSING AROUND

Look at the other menus in the menu bar and try other commands. As you experiment it would be a good idea to **keep written notes**.

Conclusions and Comments: At the end of each project you will always be asked to reach some general **conclusions** based on the results you have obtained. Try to summarize your results with special attention to the most interesting or important results. Make any **comments** you have regarding problems you experienced in doing the project or suggestions for improving the projects. If you do not have enough room on the Project Report sheets you may attach extra sheets as necessary.

Project Report 1

Getting Around in Voyager

Name_____   Student Number_____

Project Goal:

PROJECT RESULTS

1. Small command boxes

    A. Zoom in and Zoom out

    B. Dipper

    C. Saturn

    D. Galaxy

    E. Plus (+) and minus (-)

2. Object information at

    Latitude_____   Longitude_____
    Date_____   Time_____

    A. Star

B. Sun

C. Mars

3. Printouts for the year you were born

Latitude_____   Longitude_____
Date_____   Time_____

A. Star Atlas
B. Celestial Sphere
C. Local Horizon
D. Planetarium
E. Identify planets near the Sun

4. Repeat the above printouts for your birthday this year.

A. Observed differences

B. Reason for differences?

Conclusions and Comments

PROJECT 2

Looking Around the Horizon

GOAL: TO LEARN ABOUT DIURNAL MOTION AND THE HORIZON SYSTEM OF COORDINATES

ALTITUDE AND AZIMUTH

If you go out on a clear evening and look up at the sky it seems as though you are at the center of a large inverted bowl that comes down and meets the Earth in a big circle. This circle is called the **astronomical horizon.** Around the horizon are the four **cardinal points**: north, east, south, and west. Directly overhead, 90 degrees from the horizon, is the **zenith.** The point underfoot, 90 degrees below the horizon, is the **nadir.** Circles passing through the zenith and nadir are known as **vertical circles** while the circles parallel to the horizon are termed **parallels of altitude.** Because of the Earth's rotation, all celestial objects rise on the eastern horizon and set on the western horizon. The paths that objects trace out in one day are known as **diurnal circles.**

Longitude and latitude locate a place on the surface of the spherical Earth. Astronomers use similar coordinate systems to locate objects in the sky. One such set of coordinates is the **horizon system** (see Figure 2.1). The coordinates in this system are called altitude and azimuth.

Altitude is the angular distance measured from the horizon along the vertical circle through the object.

Altitude ranges from 0 to +90 degrees for objects on or above the horizon and from 0 to -90 degrees for objects below the horizon. For example, any object on the horizon has an altitude of 0 degrees, the zenith, directly overhead, has an altitude of 90 degrees, and a star midway between the horizon and zenith has an altitude of 45 degrees.

Azimuth is the angular distance measured from the north point eastward around the horizon to the vertical circle through the object.

This coordinate ranges from 0 to 360 degrees. For example, the azimuths of the north, east, south, and west points on the horizon are 0, 90, 180, and 270 degrees, respectively.

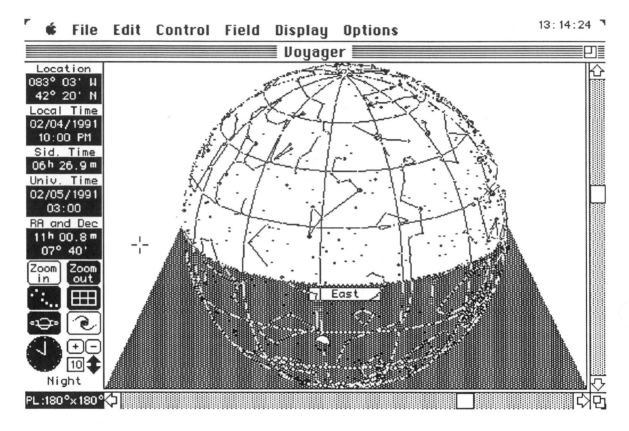

Figure 2.1 The Horizon System

SET THE LATITUDE AND LONGITUDE

To specify your observing location pull down the **Control** menu to **Set Location** and position the cursor over **Major Cities.** When the mouse button is released the **Select City** window will appear. Use the scroll bar to highlight **Detroit.** Release the mouse button and either double click on Detroit, click on the **OK** box, or press the Return key. Clicking on the **Cancel** box returns you to the Voyager screen without changing your location. Using the abbreviated instructions introduced in Project 1 the above could be written as

❏ **Control@Set Location@Major Cities**
❏ **Select City @ Detroit**
❏ **Double Click or OK or Return**

SET THE TIME OF OBSERVATION

To set your observing time, pull down the **Control** menu to **Set Time** and release the mouse button when **Local Mean Time** is highlighted. The **Set Local Mean Time** dialog box will appear. Enter the **Calendar Date** of **02/04/1991**. Change the local time to **10:00 P.M.** Choose **No** to indicate that the time is not daylight saving time. When the boxes and circles have all been filled either press the Return key or click on the **OK** box to send this information to the computer. In shortened form,

- ❑   **Control@Set Time@Local Mean Time**
- ❑   **Dialog**
        02/04/1991
        10:00 P.M.
        Daylight Saving   Time No
- ❑   **OK or Return**

THE LOCAL HORIZON SCREEN

Pull down the **Control** menu to **Sky View** and select **Local Horizon**. Make the background sky white by selecting **White Sky** from the **Display** menu. Also in the **Display** menu select **Grid Type Coarse** and **Grid Type Altazimuth**. Click on the **Constellations** (Dipper) command box. In short,

- ❑   **Control@Sky View@Local Horizon**
- ❑   **Display@White Sky**
- ❑   **Display@Grid Type@Coarse**
- ❑   **Display@Grid Type@Altazimuth**
- ❑   **Constellations On**

Use the mouse to drag the white square in the **horizontal scroll** bar at the bottom of the screen. Make sure you keep the button down as you move the mouse left and right. Notice that when the mouse button is held down a **compass** appears on the screen. The compass indicates the azimuth of the direction towards which you are looking. As you scroll horizontally the displayed azimuth changes. When you release the button the screen is redrawn to show the sky in the new direction. To make finer settings, you can click on the **left** and **right arrows** at either side of the scroll bar.

❑ **Scroll to Azimuth 90 degrees (East)**

You should see a **horizon screen** like that shown in Figure 2.2. The **Location** box should indicate the latitude and longitude of **Detroit** and the **Local Time** box should display **10:00 P.M.** The shaded portion at the bottom of the screen is your horizon and you should be looking east towards an azimuth of 90 degrees. The constellation in the middle of the screen is **Leo**, the Lion.

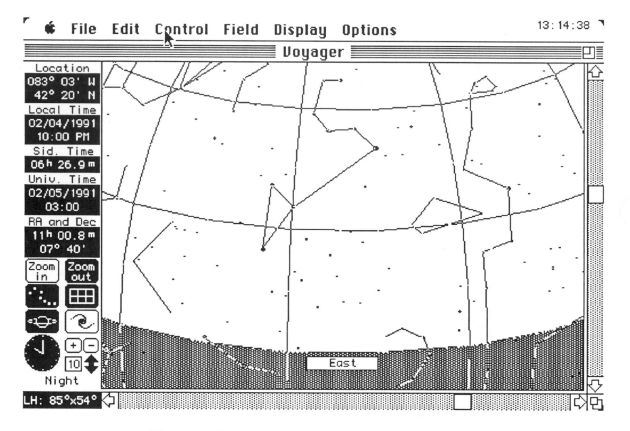

Figure 2.2   Local Horizon Screen

If Leo is not visible on your screen, use the mouse to drag the white square in the **vertical scroll** bar on the right side of the screen. When the mouse button is held down an **inclinometer** is shown in the top right-hand part of the screen. The inclinometer indicates the altitude towards which you are looking. As you scroll towards the zenith the horizon will drop out of view just as it would if you were actually outside looking up towards the zenith.

❑ **Scroll to Altitude 10 degrees**

LOOKING AROUND THE SKY

You can determine a star's altitude and azimuth by positioning the cursor over the star and clicking. The star's information box will appear. To remove the box, position the cursor in the box and click the mouse button.

Project Result 1: Choose three of the brightest stars in Leo, and record their altitudes and azimuths in the project report.

Advance the time to 10:30 by clicking three times on the **Plus** (+) command box at the bottom left corner of the screen. Each time you click on the box the time advances by 10 minutes. You can use the up/down arrow key under the **Minus (-)** box to change the **Time Increment** from 10 to another value if you wish. Clicking the **Minus (-)** box makes the sky, and time, move backward! If Leo moves off the screen, use the vertical scroll bar to reposition Leo so that it is visible.

❑   **Time Increment 10 minutes**
❑   **Plus(+) 30 Minutes**

Project Result 2: Determine the altitude and azimuth of the same three stars and record your results in the project report.

A star's information box lists its rising and setting times. Change the time to the setting time for one of the three stars. Scroll around to the western horizon and up and down in altitude until you see Leo setting.

Project Result 3: Record the altitude and azimuth of the three setting stars in the project report. Answer the questions based on your observations.

CIRCUMPOLAR STARS

Most stars rise and set each day. But some stars located close to the north celestial pole (NCP) never set and remain above the horizon for 24 hours. These are called **circumpolar** stars.

While you can observe any part of the sky using the **Local Horizon** screen it is sometimes better to step back and get a larger view of the sky. This can be done with the **Planetarium** screen (see Figure 2.1). For the best view of the circumpolar stars,

❑   **Sky View@Planetarium**
❑   **Display@Reference Points@Celestial Poles**
❑   **Display@Constellation Names**
❑   **Scroll to Azimuth 0 degrees (North)**
❑   **Scroll to Altitude 10 degrees**

You should also click on the small **Coordinate Grid** box to remove the grid. If you want to replace the grid you can click on the box at any time. All six of the small command boxes function like on/off switches.

❑   **Coordinate Grid Off**

Set the **Time Increment** to 30 minutes and while looking north advance the sky through one or two days using the **Plus** (+) box.

❑   **Time Increment 30 minutes**
❑   **Plus(+) one or two days**

Project Result 4: Answer the questions in the project report and make a printout of the circumpolar sky.

❑   **File@Print Sky Chart**

Optional Outside: Make printouts of the sky for a couple of times during each of two evenings. Compare these printouts with the actual sky. Check the altitudes and azimuths of some of the brighter stars including Polaris. Note any differences that you may observe. Are any planets or the Moon visible? If so check their positions on the star maps and note the phase of the Moon. See Appendix 4.

Project Report 2

Looking Around the Horizon

Name_____   Student Number_____

Project Goal:

PROJECT RESULTS

1. Looking east from Detroit, Michigan at 10:00 P.M.

Latitude_____   Longitude_____

	Star (in Leo)	Altitude	Azimuth
1.			
2.			
3.			

2. Looking east from Detroit, Michigan at 10:30 P.M.

	Star (in Leo)	Altitude	Azimuth
1.			
2.			
3.			

3. Looking west from Detroit, Michigan at _____(P.M./A.M.)

	Star (in Leo)	Altitude	Azimuth
1.			
2.			
3.			

Based on your observations:

A. Do the altitudes and azimuths of most stars change throughout the evening?_____

B. Describe how the altitudes and azimuths of the stars change over time. When is the altitude zero? When is it the greatest? When is the azimuth the smallest and when is it the largest?

C. Do you think that the azimuth and altitude of a star viewed at the same time by observers at different latitudes should be the same? _____ Explain your answer.

4. Circumpolar stars

A. What well known star is closest to the north celestial pole?_____

B. What constellation is it in? _____

C. What star do all other circumpolar stars seem to be moving around?_____

D. What is this star's altitude? _____

E. Printout of north circumpolar region.

F. Based on your observations, what is the relationship between the latitude and the altitude of the north celestial pole?

Hint: To verify your answer set Voyager to a different latitude, keeping the longitude and time the same as before.

Conclusions and Comments

PROJECT 3

Cruising the Zodiac

GOAL: TO LEARN ABOUT THE ZODIAC AND HOW TO LOCATE THE PLANETS, SUN, MOON, AND CONSTELLATIONS

THE SUN'S YEARLY PATH

Since the Earth moves 360 degrees around the Sun in approximately 360 days, it must move about 1 degree along its orbit each day. The Earth's revolution is what makes the Sun appear to move eastward by 1 degree per day (see Figure 3.1). Actually both the Earth and the Sun move a little less than 1 degree per day because there are 365 1/4 days in a year rather than 360 days. As viewed from the Earth, the constellations out in the Sun's direction are above the horizon during the day. But as the Sun moves eastward relative to these stars they rise earlier and earlier and eventually become visible at night. This results in different constellations being visible in the evening at different times of the year.

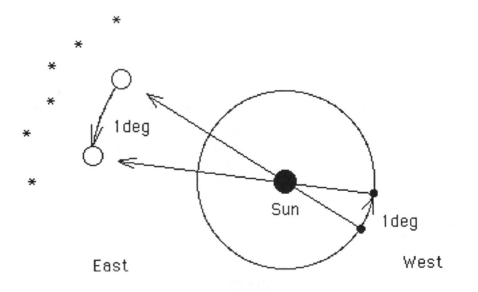

Figure 3.1 The Sun's Eastward Motion

The Sun moves through twelve constellations known as the **zodiacal constellations**. Each month it is in a different zodiacal constellation. The path that the Sun traces out in 1 year is called the **ecliptic**. The Moon and planets also appear to move eastward through the zodiacal constellations. However, the time required for this motion is not 1 year and is different for each planet.

SET THE LATITUDE AND LONGITUDE

To set your observing location,

- ❑ **Control@Set Location@Major Cities**
- ❑ **Select City@Detroit**
- ❑ **Double Click or OK or Return**

SET THE TIME OF OBSERVATION

To set your observing time,

- ❑ **Control@Set Time@Local Mean Time**
- ❑ **Dialog**
  Calendar Date Today
  10:00 P.M.
  Daylight Savings Time No
- ❑ **OK or Return**

FINDING CONSTELLATIONS

In this project you will use the **Star Atlas** screen. The celestial sphere has been flattened out into a big rectangular map, much like a map of the Earth. Viewing the sky is rather like looking at the map through a window frame. As you scroll the screen you see different parts of the sky through the window frame.

- ❑ **Control@Sky View@Star Atlas**
- ❑ **Display@White Sky**
- ❑ **Constellations On**
- ❑ **Display@Constellation Names**
- ❑ **Field@Center On Constellation**

One way to find specific constellations is to use **Center on Constellation** under the **Field** menu (see Figure 3.2).

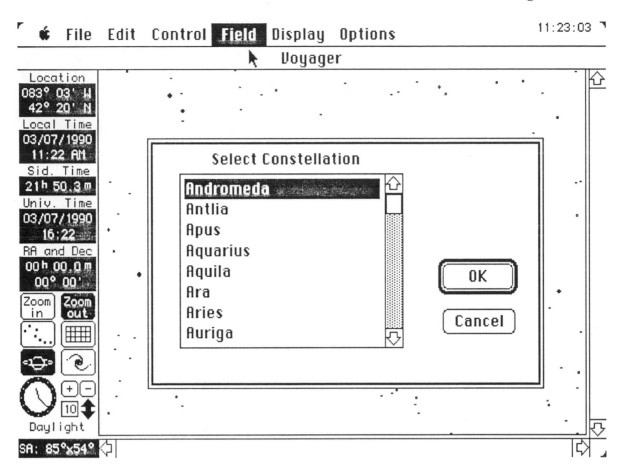

Figure 3.2.   Select Constellations Dialog Box

You can use the mouse to scroll vertically through the list of constellations. Release the mouse button when the highlighted cursor is over the desired constellation and then either **double click**, press the Return key, or click on the **OK** box. The Sky Atlas screen will be redrawn with the chosen constellation blinking in the middle and an information box at the top. To remove the constellation information box click inside the box. Click on a star in the constellation and note the rising, setting, and transit times. To remove the star information box click inside the box.

Project Result 1: Select a number of constellations and complete the constellation table in the project report.

Project Result 2: Record the names of the zodiacal constellations and the approximate month when the Sun is in each constellation. The months when the Sun is at each point along the ecliptic are marked.

FINDING THE SUN, MOON, AND PLANETS

If the command **Planet** box is white (off), click on it to turn on the Sun, Moon, and planets. Find the Sun by opening the **Field** menu and selecting **Sun** from **Center on Planet**. Click on the Sun and note its rising, setting, and transit times. Also note the zodiacal constellation that it is in. Click in the information box to close it down.

- ❑ **Planets On**
- ❑ **Field@Center On Planet@Sun**
- ❑ **Click Sun**

Project Result 3: Record this information in Planet Table I of the project report. Record the same information for the Moon and planets.

Project Result 4: Set the date ahead by about two months and record your data in Planet Table II.

Optional Outside: Make printouts of the sky for some evening and try to identify the planets that are visible. If the Moon is visible note its phase. Check the positions of the Moon and planets a few hours later and note any changes. Repeat your observations a few nights later. See Appendix 4.

Project Report 3

Cruising the Zodiac

Name_____   Student Number_____

Project Goal:

PROJECT RESULTS

1.   Finding constellations

Location _____   10:00 P.M. Date _____

		Times		
Constellation	Star	Rising	Transit	Setting
1				
2				
3				
4				
5				
6				
7				

2. The Zodiacal Constellations

Constellation	Month	Constellation	Month
1	Jan	7	Jul
2	Feb	8	Aug
3	Mar	9	Sep
4	Apr	10	Oct
5	May	11	Nov
6	Jun	12	Dec

3. Planet Table I

Location _____   10:00 P.M. Date _____

Object	Zodiacal constellation	Rising	Times Transit	Setting
Sun				
Moon				
Mercury				
Venus				
Mars				
Jupiter				
Saturn				

Hint: You can check your answers in the above table by opening the **Options** menu and selecting **Planet Positions.**

A. Do all of the objects in the above table lie in the zodiac and near the ecliptic? _____

4.   Planet Table II, two months later

Location _____   10:00 P.M. Date _____

Object	Zodiacal Constellation	Times		
		Rising	Transit	Setting
Sun				
Moon				
Mercury				
Venus				
Mars				
Jupiter				
Saturn				

   A. Do the objects still lie in the zodiac near the
ecliptic?_____

   B. Which objects have the largest change in their positions along
the zodiac?

   C. Have the rising and setting times of the objects changed
compared to what they were a few months earlier? _____

   D. What might explain the changes in position that you have
observed?

   E. What might explain the changes in rising and setting times?

Conclusions and Comments

PROJECT 4

Tracking the Sun, Moon, and Planets

GOAL: TO OBSERVE THE MOTIONS OF THE SUN, MOON, AND
PLANETS AND TO LEARN ABOUT THE EQUATORIAL SYSTEM OF
COORDINATES

RIGHT ASCENSION AND DECLINATION

While the horizon system is a local system depending on time and
location, the **equatorial system** can be used by any observer at any
time. The equatorial system is in many respects similar to the
geographical coordinate system. Latitude and longitude are independent
of time because the coordinate grid is marked out on the rotating Earth
and moves with it. Similarly, the coordinate grid of the equatorial
system can be marked out on the rotating celestial sphere (see Figure
4.1).

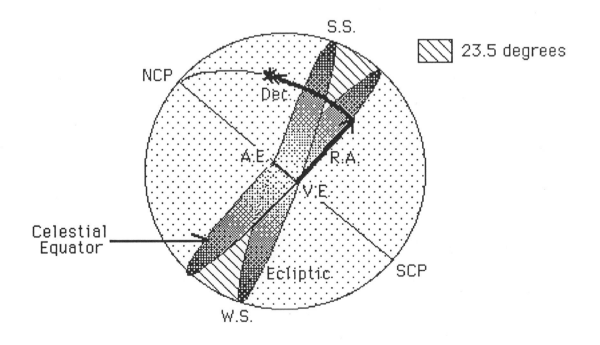

Figure 4.1   The Equatorial System of Coordinates

The coordinates of the equatorial system are called declination and right ascension.

Declination is an object's angular distance north or south of the celestial equator. It is measured along the hour circle through the object and is expressed in angular units. Declination is similar to latitude on the Earth's surface.

Right ascension is an object's angular distance from the vernal equinox. It is measured from the equinox eastward (counterclockwise) around the celestial equator to the hour circle containing the object. Right ascension is expressed in time units and is similar to longitude on the Earth's surface.

One of the major advantages of the equatorial system is that the coordinates of stars are essentially independent of time and the observer's location. This is not true, however, for solar system objects. For example, the right ascension and declination of the Sun vary continuously as it circles the ecliptic once each year. The Moon cycles through its coordinates in about one month while the time required for a planet depends on its period of revolution.

SET LOCATION AND TIME

In this project you are going to observe from Detroit, Michigan on March 21. On this date the Sun is at the vernal equinox in the constellation of Pisces and has the coordinates of that point, namely, a right ascension of 0 hours and a declination of 0 degrees. The Sun and vernal equinox will both rise at the east point on the horizon and set at the west point, spending twelve hours above and twelve hours below the horizon.

- ❑ **Control@Set Location@Major Cities**
- ❑ **Select City@Detroit**
- ❑ **Double Click or OK or Return**
- ❑ **Control@Set Time@Local Mean Time**
- ❑ **Dialog**
  03/21/1991
  12:00 P.M.
  Daylight Saving Time No
- ❑ **Double Click or OK or Return**

USING THE TRACKING SCREEN

One of the most interesting and instructive ways to view the motions of solar system objects is the **Track Planets** screen. This screen can be used with any of the standard views such as Star Atlas, Local Horizon, Planetarium, and Celestial Sphere. Figure 4.2 shows the tracking screen with the celestial sphere, the zodiacal constellations, the **ecliptic**, and the **celestial equator** dividing the sphere into two equal parts. North is above the celestial equator and south is below it. The circles parallel to the celestial equator are called **parallels of declination**. There are 10 degrees between adjacent circles.

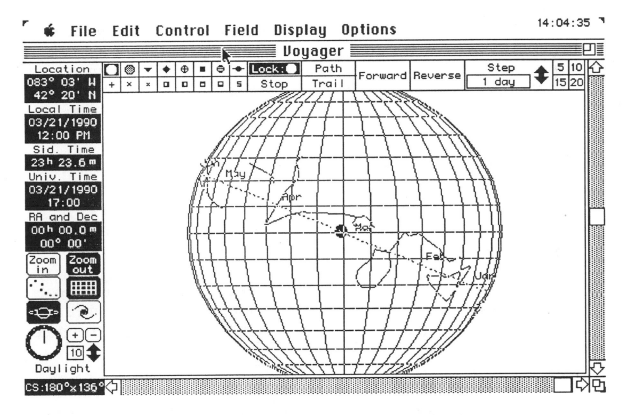

Figure 4.2. The Tracking Screen

Remember that declination ranges from 0 degrees on the equator to 90 degrees at the **north celestial pole (NCP)** and from 0 degrees to -90 degrees at the **south celestial pole (SCP)**. The poles are not visible in the figure. You can use the scroll bars to tip and rotate the celestial sphere. The circles through the NCP and SCP are called **hour circles**.

To set up the Track Planets screen,

- ❑ **Options@Track Planets**
- ❑ **Control@Sky View@Celestial Sphere**
- ❑ **Display@Zodiacal Constellations**
- ❑ **Display@Coordinate Lines@Ecliptic**
- ❑ **Display@Coordinate Lines@Celestial Equator**
- ❑ **Display@Grid Type@Equatorial**
- ❑ **Coordinate Grid On**
- ❑ **Planets On**

Below the menu bar on the tracking screen is an area containing symbols and words such as **Forward** and **Reverse**. The sixteen little **symbol boxes** contain the symbols for the Sun, Moon, nine planets, four asteroids, and the Earth's shadow. From left to right the symbols represent the Sun, Moon, Mercury, Venus, the Earth, Mars, Jupiter, and Saturn. Under these are the symbols for Uranus, Neptune, Pluto, the four asteroids, and the Earth's shadow. Notice that the planets are ordered according to their distance from the Sun.

When these symbol boxes are black the corresponding objects will be displayed on the screen. Note that in Figure 4.2 only the Sun symbol is turned on (black) and that the **Lock** box containing the Sun's symbol is also black. When the **Lock** box is black the object shown in the box will remain centered on the screen.

On your screen you will probably see most or all of the symbol boxes as black, the exception being the Earth. The Earth is turned off (white) because you are observing from the Earth and would therefore not be able to see the Earth in the sky.

When you double click on a symbol that object is centered on the screen. Double click on the Moon symbol to center it. You will notice that when you center on an object that object's symbol appears in the **Lock** box. Click the Lock box and it turns black, meaning that that object will always remain centered on the screen. When the Lock box is not black none of the objects will remain centered. Click on the Moon itself to bring up its information box.

- ❑ **Center Moon**
- ❑ **Lock Moon**
- ❑ **Click Moon**

Project Result 1: Record the Moon's data in the Data Table I of the project report. Repeat this for the other objects listed in the table.

TRACKING THE SUN

Turn off all the objects, except for the Sun, by clicking on each symbol or holding down the mouse button and dragging across the symbols so that the cursor acts like an eraser. Double click on the Sun symbol to **center** the Sun and click on the **Lock** box. Click the **up/down arrow** next to the step box until the the **Time Step** is one day. To start tracking you click the **Forward** box. You can reverse the motion by clicking the **Reverse** box. When you pull the cursor out of the Forward or Reverse box the motion will be suspended.

It should be pointed out that the speed of tracking depends not only on the chosen time step but also on the type of Mac that is being used and the number of objects, planets, stars, etc. that the machine has to redraw after each time step. Try turning off the stars by selecting **Hide Stars** in the **Display** menu.

- ❑ **Sun On**
- ❑ **Center Sun**
- ❑ **Lock Sun**
- ❑ **Time Step 1 Day**
- ❑ **Display@Hide Stars**
- ❑ **Forward/Reverse**

Click the **Forward** box and observe what happens. Suspend the motion and click on the Sun itself to bring up its information box.

- ❑ **Suspend Motion**
- ❑ **Click Sun**

Project Result 2: Record the data for the Sun in Table II. Resume tracking. Repeat this a half dozen times throughout the year, including dates around the equinoxes and solstices.

TRACKING THE MOON AND PLANETS

Turn on **Mercury** as well as the **Sun**. Center the Sun by double clicking on its symbol box. Click the **Forward** box and watch what happens.

- ❑ **Mercury On**
- ❑ **Center Sun**
- ❑ **Lock Sun**
- ❑ **Forward**

Project Result 3: Briefly describe the motion of the Sun and Mercury in the project report.

Center and lock on the **Moon** and watch it go through its phases as it moves around the zodiac. Because the Moon moves so rapidly you will probably want to use a small time step of only a couple of hours.

- ❑ **Moon On**
- ❑ **Center Moon**
- ❑ **Lock Moon**
- ❑ **Time Step 2 Hours**
- ❑ **Forward**

Project Result 4: Briefly describe the Moon's motion in the project report.

Whenever tracking is suspended you can pull down any of the menus in the menu bar of the tracking screen. Choose **Orrery** in the **Options** menu. This shows you the positions of the planets around the Sun at the instant the tracking was suspended. Experiment with the orrery, moving forward and backward in time, and zooming in and out.

Try tracking using other Voyager screens such as Star Atlas, Local Horizon, or Planetarium. To end tracking click the **Stop** box. You will be returned to the regular Voyager screen.

Project Report 4

Tracking the Sun, Moon, and Planets

Name_____   Student Number_____

Project Goal:

PROJECT RESULTS

1. Data Table I, using the tracking screen

Object	Times Rising	Transit	Setting	Above Horizon	Coordinates R.A.	Dec.
Sun						
Moon						
Mercury						
Venus						
Mars						
Jupiter						
Saturn						

Note: In the Above Horizon column record the amount of time that each object was above the horizon, that is, the difference between rising and setting times.

A. Are the coordinates and times for the Sun, Mercury, and Venus about the same?_____ Explain your answer.

B. Do objects with positive (+) declinations remain above the horizon a longer or shorter time than objects with negative (-) declinations?_____ Explain why.

C. Which objects rise before and which objects rise after the Sun rises?

Objects Before   Objects After

D. Which objects are to the west (right) and which objects are to the east (left) of the Sun?

Objects West   Objects East

2. Data Table II, tracking the Sun

Date	Rising	Times Transit	Setting	Above Horizon	Coordinates R.A.	Dec.

Note: In the Above Horizon column record the amount of time that the Sun was above the horizon, that is, the difference between rising and setting times.

A. Describe how the Sun's rising time changes throughout the year.

B. Describe how the Sun's setting time changes throughout the year.

C. Describe how the time that the Sun is above the horizon changes throughout the year.

3. Describe the motion of the Sun and Mercury. Do both move eastward along the ecliptic? Does Mercury ever "back up" and move westward?

4. Describe the motion of the Moon. Does the Moon move precisely along the ecliptic? Does it move faster or slower than the Sun? Does it go through phases as it moves?

Conclusions and Comments

Chapter 5

Orbital Motion and Precession

PROJECT 5

Inside Outer Space

GOAL: TO LEARN MORE ABOUT THE INNER FOUR PLANETS OF THE SOLAR SYSTEM

PLANETARY MOTION

The solar system consists of the Sun, nine planets and their moons as well as asteroids and comets. These objects are very different in size, composition, and structure.

As early as 300 B.C. some Greek astronomers believed that the planets traveled about the sun. This is known as the **Heliocentric Theory.** Copernicus reintroduced the Sun-centered theory centuries later.

In the early 1600s **Kepler** published his **three laws of planetary motion**. These three laws state,

(1) Each planet moves about the Sun in an elliptical orbit with the Sun at one focus.

(2) The line connecting the Sun and a planet sweeps out equal areas in equal intervals of time.

(3) The semi-major axis cubed is equal to the period of revolution squared.

The first two laws imply that a planet's orbital velocity and distance from the Sun continually change. Specifically, a planet moves fastest when it is closest to the Sun and slowest when it is farthest from the Sun. Kepler's third law can be written as

$$a^3 = p^2$$

where **a** is the **semi-major axis** of the planet's orbit measured in **Astronomical Units** (AU) and **P** is the **sidereal period** expressed in years.

About 60 years later Newton explained these motions in terms of his **Universal Law of Gravity**,

$$F = \frac{GmM}{D^2}$$

where **F** is the gravitational force of attraction between the masses **m** and **M, D** is the distance between their centers, and **G** is the **universal gravitational constant.**

When a mass, m, is dropped near the Earth's surface this force produces an acceleration of 9.8 meters per second per second. The gravitational acceleration, g, does not depend on the mass, m, of the falling object,

$$g = \frac{GM}{R^2}$$

As before, **G** is the universal gravitational constant, but **M** now represents the mass of the Earth and **R** is its radius. Notice that the gravitational acceleration, or as it is sometimes known, the **surface gravity**, depends only upon the mass and radius of the attracting object. Using the appropriate values of M and R, the surface gravity of any object can be calculated from this formula. The Moon's surface gravity is only one-sixth that of the Earth. Therefore an object weighing 180 pounds on the Earth would weigh only 30 pounds on the Moon.

Today, more than three centuries later, the laws of Kepler and Newton are still used to describe and predict the motions of planets. In this project you will explore the motions and some of the physical properties of the four planets closest to the Sun.

SET LOCATION AND TIME

With Voyager you can view the solar system not only from the Earth's surface but from any point in space. To see the solar system as if you were looking down on it from north of the ecliptic,

- ❑ **Control@Set Time@Universal Time**
- ❑ **Dialog**
  Calendar Date Today
  21:00 hours
- ❑ **OK or Return**
- ❑ **Options@Observe From Point.**
- ❑ **Heliocentric Longitude 0 degrees**
- ❑ **Heliocentric Latitude 90 degrees**
- ❑ **Distance 3.5 A.U.**

PHYSICAL PROPERTIES

With Voyager it is easy to collect some rather important data concerning the physical properties of the planets.

- ❑ **Options@Track Planets**
- ❑ **Objects Off**
- ❑ **Sun, Mercury, Venus, Earth, and Mars On**
- ❑ **Center Sun**
- ❑ **Lock Sun**

Project Result 1: Click on each of the four displayed planets and the Sun to bring up their information boxes. Record your data in the Inner Planet Data table of the project and answer the related questions.

SEE HOW THEY RUN

It is both fascinating and instructive to watch the planets as they orbit the Sun.

- ❑ **Display@Hide Stars**
- ❑ **Time Step 1 week**
- ❑ **Path On**
- ❑ **Forward**

Project Result 2: Observe the planetary motion through one or two complete revolutions of Mars and make a white sky printout. Label the Sun, Mercury, Venus, Earth, and Mars and answer the related questions in the project report.

You can change your point of view by using the up/down **location arrows** at the top left of the screen. When the cursor is positioned on an arrow hold the mouse button down until the displayed value is the one you want.

Project Result 3: Try changing the heliocentric latitude to 45 and 0 degrees, watching the planetary motion from each of these positions. Observe the motion through one or two complete revolutions of Mars and make a white sky printout for these heliocentric latitudes. Label the Sun, Mercury, Venus, Earth, and Mars and answer the related questions in the project report.

Project Report 5

Inside Outer Space

Name_____ Student Number_____

Project Goal:

PROJECT RESULTS

1. Inner Planet Data

Planet	Mercury	Venus	Earth	Mars	Sun
Mass					
Diameter					
Density					
Gravity					
Per of Rev					XXX
Per of Rot					
Sun Distance					XXX

   A. What unit of measurement is being used for

     (1) Mass _____

(2) Diameter_____

(3) Density_____

(4) Surface gravity_____

(5) Period of revolution_____

(6) Period of rotation_____

(7) Distance from the Sun_____

B. Which planet has the greatest radius?_____

C. Which planet has the greatest mass? _____

D. Which planet has the greatest density? _____

E. Which planet has the greatest surface gravity?

_____

F. Which two planets have nearly equal surface gravities? Since the planets are different sizes, how can they have the same surface gravity?

G. Verify Kepler's third law.

Planet	a (AU)	P (years)	a^3	P^2
Mercury				
Venus				
Earth				
Mars				

2. Planetary motions

　　A. Labeled printout for heliocentric latitude 90 degrees

　　B. Do the inner planets orbit the Sun clockwise or counterclockwise as viewed from north of the ecliptic?

　　_____

　　C. Which planet has the shortest period of revolution?

　　_____

3. Heliocentric latitudes 45 and 0 degrees

　　A. Labeled printouts

　　B. Do the inner planets orbit the Sun in the same plane?

　　_____

Conclusions and Comments

PROJECT 6

Outside Inner Space

GOAL: TO LEARN MORE ABOUT THE OUTER FIVE PLANETS OF THE SOLAR SYSTEM

INTRODUCTION

Because Mercury, Venus, Mars, Jupiter, and Saturn are all visible to the naked eye they have been observed for many centuries. Ancient astronomers noticed that these five "stars" were different than other stars in that they seemed to move along the ecliptic. For this reason they called them planets, which means wanderers. After the invention of the telescope in 1608 three other wanderers were discovered, namely Uranus, discovered in 1781, Neptune, discovered in 1846, and Pluto, which was discovered in 1930.

Jupiter, Saturn, Uranus, and Neptune are very similar in size, composition and structure and are sometimes called the **gas giants**. But the most recently discovered planet, Pluto, is very different. In this project you will explore the similarities and differences between the five outer planets of the solar system.

SET LOCATION AND TIME

With Voyager you can view the solar system not only from the Earth's surface but from any point in space. To see the solar system as if you were looking down on it from north of the ecliptic,

- ❏ Control@Set Time@Local Mean Time
- ❏ Dialog
  Calendar Date 1700 A.D.
  21:00 hours
- ❏ OK or Return
- ❏ Options@Observe From Point
- ❏ Heliocentric Longitude 0 degrees
- ❏ Heliocentric Latitude 90 degrees
- ❏ Distance 100 AU

PHYSICAL PROPERTIES

With Voyager it is easy to collect some rather important data concerning the physical properties of the planets.

- ❑　**Options@Track Planets**
- ❑　**Objects Off**
- ❑　**Sun, Jupiter, and Saturn On**
- ❑　**Uranus, Neptune, and Pluto On**
- ❑　**Center Sun**
- ❑　**Lock Sun**

Project Result 1: Click on each of the five displayed planets and the Sun to bring up their information boxes. Record your data in the Outer Planet Data table of the project report and answer the related questions.

SEE HOW THEY RUN

It is both fascinating and instructive to watch these planets as they orbit the Sun.

- ❑　**Display@Hide Stars**
- ❑　**Time Step 4 years**
- ❑　**Path On**
- ❑　**Forward**

Project Result 2: Observe the planetary motion through at least one complete revolution of Pluto and make a white sky printout. Label the Sun and planets and answer the related questions in the project report.

Project Result 3: You can change your point of view by using the up/down **location arrows** at the top left of the screen. When the cursor is positioned on an arrow hold the mouse button down until the displayed value is the one you want. Try changing the heliocentric latitude to 45, 20, and 7 degrees, watching the planetary motion from each of these positions. Observe the motion through one or two complete revolutions of Pluto and make a white sky printout for heliocentric latitude 7 degrees.

Project Report 6

Outside Inner Space

Name_____   Student Number_____

Project Goal:

PROJECT RESULTS

1. Outer Planet Data

Planet	Jupiter	Saturn	Neptune	Uranus	Pluto	Sun
Mass						
Diameter						
Density						
Gravity						
Per of Rev						XXX
Per of Rot						
Sun Distance						XXX

    A. Which of the outer planets has the:

        (1) Largest diameter? _____

(2) Greatest mass? _____

(3) Highest density? _____

B. Compare the diameters and masses of the five outer planets.
Which planet in this group is not a gas giant? _____

C. The density of water is 1 gram per cubic centimeter.   Which
outer planet is less dense than water? _____

D. Do all of the gas giants have a surface gravity greater than
Earth's? _____

F. Verify Kepler's third law

Planet	a (AU)	P (years)	a^3	p^2
Jupiter				
Saturn				
Neptune				
Uranus				
Pluto				

2. Planetary motions

A. Printout with Sun and planets labeled

B. Do the outer planets orbit the Sun in a clockwise or
counterclockwise direction as viewed from north of the
ecliptic?_____

Is this the same as for the inner planets? _____

3.   Heliocentric latitude 7 degrees.

   A. Labeled printout

   B. Do the outer planets orbit the Sun in the same plane? _____ If not, which planet has its orbital plane tilted with respect to the others? _____

   C. At times Pluto is closer to the Sun than Neptune. Which of these two planets is currently closer to the Sun? _____

   D. Estimate the inclination of Pluto's orbital plane relative to the ecliptic plane._____

Conclusions and Comments

PROJECT 7

Spinning Like a Top

GOAL: TO INVESTIGATE THE PRECESSION OF THE EQUINOXES

EQUINOXES AND SOLSTICES

The Earth's revolution about the Sun makes the Sun appear to move eastward, along the ecliptic. Each month the Sun is in a different zodiacal constellation. The circle labeled **Ecliptic** in Figure 7.1 shows the Sun's yearly path through the zodiacal constellations. The ecliptic is actually the Earth's orbital plane extended out to the sky. The ecliptic is inclined to the celestial equator by 23.5 degrees because the Earth's equator is tipped 23.5 degrees relative to its orbital plane.

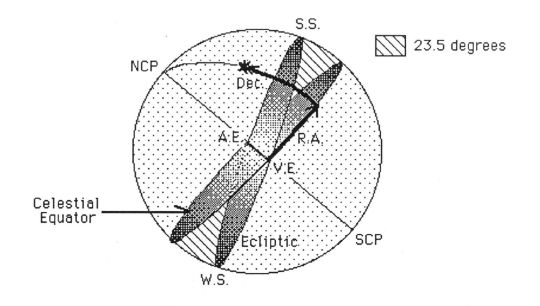

Figure 7.1   The Equinoxes

The Sun moves counterclockwise (eastward) around the ecliptic, travelling about one degree per day. On March 21 it is at the point marked V.E. On June 21 it is at point S.S. On September 21 the Sun is at point A.E. and on December 21 it is at point W.S. These points are called the **vernal equinox**, the **summer solstice**, the **autumnal equinox**, and the **winter solstice**, respectively.

While we often think of the equinoxes and solstices as dates they are really points on the ecliptic. These points, like celestial objects, have a diurnal motion. The vernal equinox rises at the east point and sets at the west point on the horizon every day in the year. However, the Sun is at the vernal equinox only on March 21. On this date the Sun, along with the the equinox, rises at the east point and sets at the west point.

PRECESSION OF THE EQUINOXES

The vernal equinox is presently in the zodiacal constellation of **Pisces**. At the beginning of spring the Sun is also in this constellation. But this has not always been the case. Thousands of years ago the vernal equinox was in the constellation of Aries the Ram and even today this point is sometimes known as the First Point of Aries. In about 150 BC the Greek astronomer Hipparchus discovered that the vernal and autumnal equinoxes move slowly westward along the ecliptic. The rate of movement is about 50.26 seconds of arc per year. At this rate the equinoxes complete one cycle around the ecliptic in about 25,800 years. This is known as the **precession of the equinoxes.**

Precession results from the Earth's axis of rotation wobbling like a spinning top. One wobble takes about 25,800 years to complete. This motion is caused primarily by the gravitational pull of the Sun and Moon on the Earth's equatorial bulge. Since the Earth's axis points to the north (NCP) and south (SCP) celestial poles, these poles also precess. This means that the star we call the North Star changes over time. Polaris is presently the North Star and lies within 0.5 degrees of the NCP, but back when the pyramids were built a star called Thuben, in the constellation of Draco the Dragon, was the North Star. A few thousand years from now Vega in the constellation of Lyra will be the North Star.

The equatorial system of coordinates is based upon the location of the vernal equinox on the celestial sphere. For instance the coordinate of right ascension is measured from this point. The movement of the vernal equinox, therefore, causes the coordinate of right ascension to change over time. Perhaps less obviously, an object's declination also changes. Because this change is caused by precession it takes place over a period of 25,800 years. Although small over the lifetime of an individual, this change accumulates over the years and must be taken into account not only in specifying the locations of objects but also in the design of solar calendars.

To correctly specify the location of an object on the celestial sphere one must give not only its right ascension and declination, but also the year, known as the **epoch**, for which those coordinates apply. Star charts and star catalogs always indicate the epoch upon which they are based. For example they may be for epoch 1950, epoch 2000, or indeed any year as long as it is noted.

SET LOCATION AND TIME

You can use the location set by the program or enter your own location.

- ❏ **Control@Set Time@Universal Time**
- ❏ **Dialog**
  03/21/2000
  12:00 hours
- ❏ **OK or Return**

DIFFERENT EPOCHS

In this project you will explore some of the changes brought about due to the precession of the Earth's axis of rotation.

- ❏ **Control@Sky View@Star Atlas**
- ❏ **Display@Coordinate Lines@Ecliptic**
- ❏ **Display@Coordinate Lines@Celestial Equator**
- ❏ **Display@Zodiacal Constellations**
- ❏ **Display@Constellation Names**
- ❏ **Field@Center on Planet@Sun**
- ❏ **Options@Precession Cycle**
- ❏ **Dialog**
  Time Step 500 years

Project Result 1: Record the name of the constellation that the Sun is closest to as well as the other requested data in the Sun/VE data table of the project report. Forward to the next epoch and record the same data. Reset the date to **03/21/2000** and the time to **12:00 hours**. Center and click on **Vega** and record the data requested in the Vega data table. Forward to the next epoch and record the same data.

THE CHANGING CELESTIAL POLE

Precession results in different stars becoming the **Pole Star**, or **North Star.** To view this change reset the date to **03/21/2000**, the time to **12:00 hours**, and use the vertical scroll bar to set the declination to **90 degrees.** Then,

- ❏ **Constellations On**
- ❏ **Display@Grid Type@Coarse**
- ❏ **Display@Grid Type@Equatorial**
- ❏ **Options@Precession Cycle**
- ❏ **Poles On**
- ❏ **Forward**

Project Result 2: Center and click on **Polaris** and record the data requested in the Polaris data table. Forward to the next epoch and record the same data. Make a white sky printout for each epoch. Before you make the printout you might wish to turn the coordinate grid off and recenter the circle of pole locations using the scroll bars. On each printout label the

- **(1)** stars Polaris and Vega
- **(2)** North celestial pole locations with the year of each epoch
- **(3)** North ecliptic pole, which is the center of the pole locations circle

Project Report 7

Spinning Like a Top

Name_____   Student Number_____

Project Goal:

PROJECT RESULTS

1. Precession of the equinoxes

    A. Sun/VE data

Object	Epoch	Constellation	Declination	R. A.
Sun/VE	2000 A.D.			
Sun/VE	15000 A.D.			
Sun/VE	28000 A.D.			

    B. Vega data

Object	Epoch	Const.	Dec	R. A.	Rising	Setting
					Times	
Vega	2000 A.D.					
Vega	15000 A.D.					
Vega	28000 A.D.					

(1) Do the declination and right ascension of the Sun and vernal equinox change with time?_____ Explain why.

(2) Do the declination and right ascension of Vega change with time?_____ Explain why.

(3) Do the rising and setting times of Vega change with time?_____ Explain why.

2. Precession of the celestial poles

   A. Labeled printouts 2000, 15000, and 28000 A.D.

   B. Polaris data

Object	Epoch	Const.	Dec.	R. A.	Times Rising	Setting
Polaris	2000 A.D.					
Polaris	15000 A.D.					
Polaris	28000 A.D.					

(1) Do the declination and right ascension of Polaris change with time?_____ Explain why.

(2) Do the rising and setting times of Polaris change with time?_____ Explain why.

(3) What very bright star is close to the North Celestial Pole in the year 15,000 AD? _____

(4) In your lifetime would you expect to see a change to a new pole star? _____ Explain why.

Conclusions and Comments

Chapter 6

Seasons and Time

PROJECT 8

Speaking of Seasons

GOAL: TO LEARN MORE ABOUT THE SEASONS AND OBSERVE THE DAILY MOTION OF THE SUN FROM DIFFERENT LATITUDES

SEASONS AND THE SUN

As you have discovered, the Sun appears to move eastward around the ecliptic once each year. This yearly motion results from the Earth's revolution about the Sun. The Sun also moves north and south of the celestial equator. On the date of the **summer solstice** (June 21) the Sun is north of the celestial equator and has a declination of 23.5 degrees while, on the date of the **winter solstice** (December 21), the Sun is south of the celestial equator and has a declination of -23.5 degrees (see Figure 8.1).

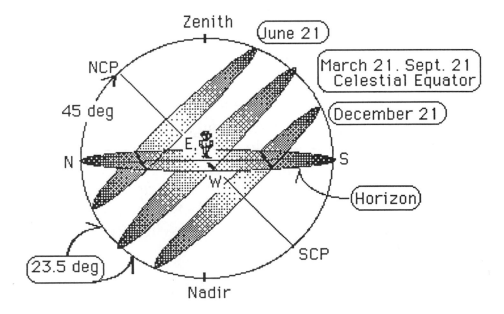

Figure 8.1 The North-South Motion of the Sun

The Sun moves north and south because the Earth's rotational axis is inclined by 23.5 degrees to its orbital plane (see Figure 8.2).

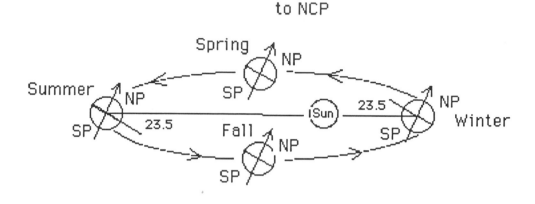

Figure 8.2   Inclination of the Earth's Axis

This north-south motion causes the Sun's rising and setting azimuths, the length of the day, and the Sun's noon altitude to change throughout the year. When the Sun is at the summer solstice it rises farthest north of east, days are longer than nights, and the noon altitude of the Sun is greatest. At the winter solstice the Sun rises farthest south of east, days are shorter than nights, and the Sun's noon altitude is the smallest of any time in the year.

Because of the Sun's north-south motion the angle that the Sun's rays strike the Earth changes throughout the year. During the summer the rays come in more nearly perpendicularly than they do in the winter. Consequently, in the summer the energy in a cylindrical bundle of rays goes into heating a smaller area than it does in the winter (see Figure 8.3). Thus, the warming effect of the Sun's rays is greater in the summer than in the winter and it is this difference in heating efficiency that results in the seasons.

If the Earth's rotational axis were not inclined to the orbital plane the Sun would rise at the east point and set at the west point each day, and each day it would remain above the horizon for 12 hours. We would not have seasons as we know them. It is the 23.5 degree inclination of the Earth's axis of rotation that produces the seasons.

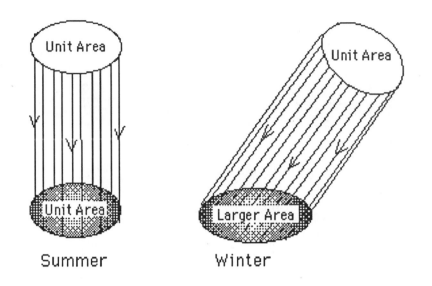

Figure 8.3   The Warming Effect of the Sun's Rays

SET LOCATION AND TIME

In this project you will set your location using **World Map** (Figure 8.4) rather than Major Cities. To choose the World Map,

❏   **Control@Set Location@World Map**

Move the mouse cursor onto the map and notice the changing coordinates displayed in the lower left-hand corner of the screen. If you click the mouse button anywhere on the map, the map will be redrawn with the new position centered on the cursor. You can click on the **OK** box to enter this position. If you click on the **Show Cities** button all of the major cities will be shown as dots on the map. Clicking on the **Magnify 8x** button will show the names of the major cities.

You can also specify a location by using the dialog box in the upper right-hand corner of the screen. Use this box to enter a **longitude** of 75 degrees west, a **latitude** of 45 degrees north, and a **time zone** of 5 hours.

❏   **World Map Dialog**
        Longitude 75 deg. W
        Latitude 45 deg. N
        Time Zone 5 Hours
❏   **Double Click or OK or Return**

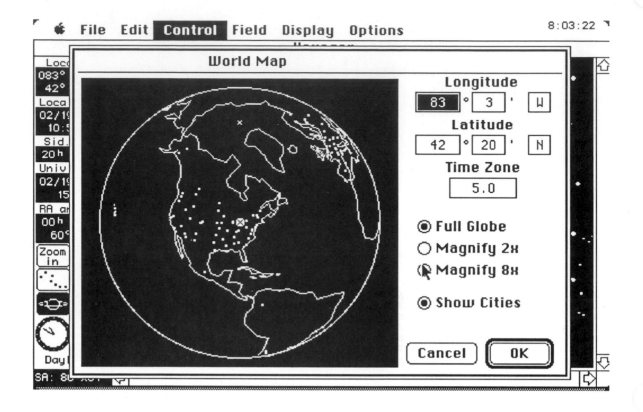

Figure 8.4 World Map Screen

To set the time for this project,

❑   **Control@Set Time@Local Mean Time**
❑   **Dialog**
       03/21/1991
       12:00 P.M.
       Daylight Savings Time No
❑   **Double Click or OK or Return**

VIEWING SEASONS FROM THE SUN

With Voyager you can view the sky from anywhere in the solar system. In this section you will place yourself on the Sun and watch the seasons as they occur on Earth!

❑   **Display@Major Planets@Planet Images**
❑   **Earth Disk On**
❑   **OK**

❑   **Display@Major Planets@Planet Phases On**
❑   **Display@Major Planets@Planet Grids On**
❑   **Control@SkyView@Solar System**
❑   **Options@Observe from Planets@Sun**
❑   **Options@Track Planets**
❑   **Sun, Moon, Planets Off**
❑   **Earth On**
❑   **Center Earth**
❑   **Lock Earth**
❑   **Zoom In**
❑   **Display@Hide Stars**
❑   **Display@White Sky**
❑   **Time Step 1 Week**
❑   **Forward**

Note that when **Planet Phases** and **Grids** are turned on a check will appear next to these items. Zoom in until you can see the continents and coordinate grid but don't make the Earth so large that you can't see the entire Earth. Remember that if you want to stop the tracking you need only pull the cursor from the **Forward** box and if you want to reverse the motion and go backwards in time you click the **Reverse** box. As the tracking proceeds pay particular attention to which hemisphere of the Earth (north or south) is pointing towards you. Keep in mind that you are viewing the Earth from the Sun.

Project Result 1: Stop the tracking when the date is about March 21, June 21, September 21, and December 21. Make a printout for each of these four dates. On each printout label the north and south poles of the Earth and indicate the season occurring in both the northern and southern hemispheres.

When you have finished viewing the Earth's seasons,

❑   **Click Stop**
❑   **Options@Return to Earth**
❑   **Control@Sky View@Planetarium**
❑   **Scroll to South Point**

You are now back on the Earth and ready to start the next part of this project.

THE SUN'S CHANGING NOON ALTITUDE

In this section you will observe the Sun at noon from midlatitude, the north pole, and the equator on the dates of the equinoxes and solstices.

- ❑ Control@Set Location@World Map
- ❑ World Map
- ❑ Dialog
  Longitude 75 deg. W
  Latitude 45 deg. N
  Time Zone 5 Hours
- ❑ Double Click or OK or Return
- ❑ Control@Set Time@Local Mean Time
- ❑ Dialog
  03/21/1991
  12:00 P.M.
  Daylight Savings Time No
- ❑ Double Click or OK or Return
- ❑ Field@Center on Planet@Sun
- ❑ Click Sun

Project Result 2: Record the information requested in the midlatitude table of the project report and then repeat for June 21, September 21, and December 21.

Project Result 3: Repeat the above instructions for latitude 90 degrees north. Record the information in the north pole table of the project report.

Project Result 4: Repeat the above instructions for latitude 0 degrees. Record the information in the equator table of the project report.

The noon altitude of the Sun depends on the observer's latitude and the declination of the Sun,

noon altitude of Sun = 90 - latitude + declination

Use this formula to check the results of your observations and record your computed altitude in the CompAlt column of each table.

Project Report 8

Speaking of Seasons

Name_____ Student Number_____

Project Goal:

PROJECT RESULTS

1. Printouts of the Earth for March 21, June 21, September 21, and December 21. On each printout label the north and south poles of the Earth and indicate the season occurring in both the northern and southern hemispheres.

2. Sun at noon viewed from midlatitude (45 degrees north)

Date	Times Rising	Setting	Sun Dec.	Noon ObsAlt	CompAlt
March 21					
June 21					
September 21					
December 21					

3.   Sun at noon viewed from the north pole (90 degrees North)

Date	Times		Sun	Noon	
	Rising	Setting	Dec.	ObsAlt	CompAlt
March 21					
June 21					
September 21					
December 21					

4.   Sun at noon viewed from the equator (0 degrees)

Date	Times		Sun	Noon	
	Rising	Setting	Dec.	ObsAlt	CompAlt
March 21					
June 21					
September 21					
December 21					

A. On what date and at what latitude does the Sun have its largest noon altitude?

Latitude_____   Date_____   Alt_____

B. On what date and at what latitude does the Sun rise the earliest?

Latitude_____   Date_____   Rise_____

Conclusions and Comments

PROJECT 9

Time Marches On

GOAL: TO LEARN ABOUT DIFFERENT TYPES OF LOCAL TIMES AND HOW THEY RELATE TO LONGITUDE

TYPES OF TIME

There are many different types of time. The time told by the Sun is called local apparent time (**LAT**). Other kinds of time include local mean time (**LMT**) and local sidereal time (**LST**).

At any instant, each of these local times depends on a chosen celestial object's position relative to the observer's astronomical meridian. This position is given by the local hour angle (**LHA**), which is simply how far an object is to the west of an observer's meridian (see Figure 9.1).

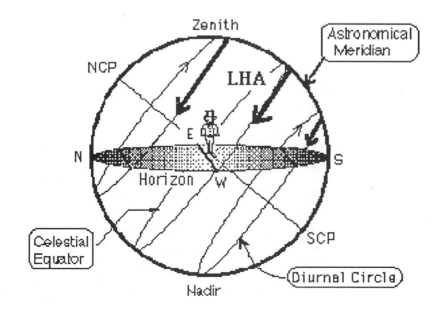

Figure 9.1 Local Hour Angle

At upper transit an object's LHA is 0 hours. Six hours later, the object will be 6 hours to the west of the astronomical meridian and have an LHA of 6 hours. Twelve hours after upper transit the object will be at lower transit and have an LHA of 12 hours. Thus, an object's LHA can also be thought of as the number of hours that have passed since it was at upper transit. It should be noted that an object to the east of the meridian is sometimes said to have a negative LHA. That is, 18 hours is equivalent to a minus (-) 6 hours.

The following formulas can be used to compute the different types of local times,

1. $LAT = LHA_{Sun} + 12$ **hours**

2. $LMT = LHA_{Mean\ Sun} + 12$ **hours**

3. $LST = LHA_{vernal\ equinox}$

Recall that the **Mean Sun** is a fictitious Sun that moves along the celestial equator with the real Sun's average (mean) speed.

No matter what the type of time, there are always 24 hours in 1 **day**, which is the time interval between two successive meridian crossings of a chosen celestial object. If a computed time is greater than 24 hours you should subtract 24 hours from the time, and if a computed time is negative, 24 hours should be added to the time.

When the Sun is at upper transit on a particular observer's astronomical meridian its LHA is 0 hours and the LAT is 12 noon. But for an observer 1 hour to the west in longitude, the Sun would be 1 hour from upper transit, to the east of this observer's meridian, and the LAT would be 11 A.M. The difference between the local times of two observers is exactly equal to the difference in their longitudes,

difference in longitude = difference in local time

Because the local time to the west of any particular observer is earlier by an amount equal to the longitude difference, the time to the west (LT_{west}) is found by subtracting the longitude difference from the observer's local time (LT_{obs}),

$$LT_{west} = LT_{obs} - \text{longitude difference}$$

However, the longitude difference is added to find the time to the east,

$$LT_{east} = LT_{obs} + \text{longitude difference}$$

In the above equations the local time (LT) can be LAT, LMT, or LST.

Longitude is measured east and west of the **Prime Meridian** passing through **Greenwich**, England. Since the continental United States lies to the west of Greenwich, the time everywhere in the U.S. is earlier than that at Greenwich, while at points to the east of Greenwich the time is later. The LMT at Greenwich is often called Universal Time (**UT**).

Nowadays it is obviously impractical for everyone to keep their own local time so the world has been divided into a number of **standard time zones**, each covering 1 hour (15 degrees) of longitude. The meridian passing through the center of each zone is called the **standard time meridian**. In the U.S. the longitudes of the standard time meridians are 5 hours west, 6 hours west, 7 hours west, and 8 hours west. The corresponding time zones are Eastern Standard, Central Standard, Mountain Standard, and Pacific Standard. The times kept in these zones are called Eastern Standard Time (**EST**), Central Standard Time (**CST**), Mountain Standard Time (**MST**), and Pacific Standard Time (**PST**), respectively.

Standard time is defined as the local mean time of the standard time meridian. Within each zone everyone agrees to keep the LMT of the zone's standard time meridian. For example, in the EST zone each watch is set to read the LMT of an observer at 5 hours west longitude.

Optional Outside: A sundial keeps local apparent time. Appendix 2 describes how to build and use a sundial. You can discover a great deal about time by constructing a sundial and learning about the oldest and most natural way of keeping time.

SET LOCATION AND TIME

In this project you will begin your observations at London, England. The reason for this choice is that the **Prime Meridian** (0 hours longitude) passes through Greenwich, which is just outside of London.

❑   **Control@Set Location@Major Cities**
❑   **Select City@London**
❑   **Double Click or OK or Return**
❑   **Control@Set Time@Local Mean Time**
❑   **Dialog**
         03/21/1991
         12:00 P.M.
         Daylight Savings Time No
❑   **Double Click or OK or Return**

TIME AND HOUR ANGLE

Local times are based on the local hour angle of either the Sun, Mean Sun, or vernal equinox. In the following activity you are going to investigate the relationship between local time and hour angle.

❑   **Control@SkyView@Local Horizon**
❑   **Scroll to South**
❑   **Display@Coordinate Lines@Meridian**
❑   **Click Sun**

Project Result 1: Record the data requested in the Local Time table of the project report. Besides the Sun, choose any three other objects to complete the table.

It is important to note that the time referred to in Voyager as local mean time is not the LMT that has been discussed above. What Voyager refers to as local mean time is what is more often called **standard time (ST)** or **watch time.**

TIME AND LONGITUDE

You are next going to investigate the relationship between time and longitude. Make sure that you are still located in **London,** that the date is **March 21**, and that the Greenwich time (UT) is **12 P.M. (Noon)**.

Project Result 2: Use **Major Cities** to set your location to London, Philadelphia, Chicago, Denver, and San Francisco. Record your data in the Longitude and Time table of the project report. When you change cities **do not** change the local time to noon. Use the local time that results from the longitude change.

The cities of Philadelphia, Chicago, Denver, and San Francisco are in the Eastern Standard, Central Standard, Mountain Standard, and Pacific Standard time zones, respectively.

Project Report 9

Time Marches On

Name_____   Student Number_____

Project Goal:

PROJECT RESULTS

1.   Local time and hour angle

Location: London, England   **Latitude:** $51^0 30'$ **Longitude:** 0 hr

Date: March 21, 19____   UT_____ (AM or PM)
                                     LST_____

Object	Transit Time	LHA	R.A.	R.A. + LHA
1. Sun				
2.				
3.				
4.				

Hint: UT and LST are given in the time boxes on the left of the screen. To find the local hour angle recall that it is the number of hours that have passed since an object was at upper transit or until an object will be at upper transit. That is, the local hour angle of an object is equal to the local time minus the transit time.

A. Calculate the LAT.

LAT = _____

B. Study the data recorded in the above table and state a general relationship between LST, R.A., and LHA.

LST = _____

2. Longitude and time table

Location	Long.	Standard Time(ST)	LST	Diff. LST	Diff. ST	Diff. Long
London	0 hr W	12 PM		0 hr	0 hr	0 hr
Philadelphia	5 hr W					5 hr
Chicago	5.8 hr W					5.8 hr
Denver	7 hr W					7 hr
San Francisco	8.2 hr W					8.2 hr

Hint: The diff. local sidereal time (LST), diff. standard time (ST), and diff. longitude (long.) are the differences between the London values and the corresponding values at each of the other cities.

A. Is the difference in longitude between London and each of the other cities equal to the difference in local sidereal times?_____

B. Why isn't the difference in longitude between London and each of the other cities equal to the difference in standard times?

Conclusions and Comments

PROJECT 10

The Sun's Figure Eight

GOAL: TO LEARN MORE ABOUT THE EQUATION OF TIME

THE SUN'S NONUNIFORM MOTION

Many centuries ago it was discovered that the Sun does not move uniformly along the ecliptic. This nonuniform motion is partly due to the fact that the Earth's orbital speed changes (Kepler's second law). The Earth moves fastest in the winter when it is closest to the Sun and slowest in the summer when it is farthest from the Sun. As the Earth's orbital speed changes, so does the apparent eastward motion of the Sun. Another reason for the nonuniformity is the 23.5 degree inclination of the Earth's rotational axis to the orbital plane.

The nonuniform motion of the Sun causes local apparent time (**LAT**) to be nonuniform. For example, on those dates when the Sun moves more than one degree eastward the time between lower transits is greater than usual and the day is longer. The reverse is the case on dates when the Sun moves less than one degree. So local apparent days, hours, minutes, and seconds are not always the same length. The Mean Sun was invented to eliminate this problem. The Mean Sun moves eastward along the celestial equator, rather than along the ecliptic, and it moves with the real Sun's average (mean) speed. Thus, the Mean Sun moves uniformly and this, in turn, insures that local mean time (**LMT**) is also uniform.

THE EQUATION OF TIME

Local apparent and local mean times are related by the **equation of time (E)**, which is defined as the difference between local apparent time and local mean time,

$$E = LAT - LMT$$

Because of its nonuniform motion, the actual Sun is sometimes ahead of and sometimes behind the Mean Sun. If the Sun is ahead of the Mean

Sun it will be at upper transit before the Mean Sun, LAT will be greater than LMT, and E will be positive. When LAT is less than LMT, E is negative and the Sun transits after the Mean Sun. The equation of time ranges between about plus and minus 16 minutes. The values of E can be computed and repeat themselves each year.

SET LOCATION AND TIME

In this project you will begin your observations at London, England. The reason for this choice is that the **Prime Meridian** (0 hours longitude) passes through Greenwich, which is just outside of London.

- ❑   **Control@Set Location@Major Cities**
- ❑   **Select City@London**
- ❑   **Double Click or OK or Return**
- ❑   **Control@Set Time@Local Mean Time**
- ❑   **Dialog**
  03/21/19??
  12:00 P.M.
  Daylight Savings Time No
- ❑   **Double Click or OK or Return**

VIEWING THE SUN'S FIGURE EIGHT

The figure eight motion of the Sun that you are about to observe is called the **analemma**. The analemma shows how the equation of time varies throughout the year. The equation of time is **positive** on the right side of the analemma and **negative** on the left side. Four times in the year the equation of time is zero. These times occur at the top, middle, and bottom of the figure eight.

- ❑   **Control@SkyView@Planetarium**
- ❑   **Display@Coordinate Lines@Meridian**
- ❑   **Display@Hide Stars**
- ❑   **Display@White Sky**
- ❑   **Options@Track Planets**
- ❑   **Planets Off**
- ❑   **Sun On**

Clicking on each object symbol will turn the object off. You can also hold the mouse button down and drag across the object symbols.

As long as the mouse button is held down the cursor acts as an eraser turning the black (on) symbols off (white). Double clicking on a symbol will center the object.

- ❑ **Center Sun**
- ❑ **Scroll to South**
- ❑ **Path On**
- ❑ **Time Step 1 Week**
- ❑ **Forward**

Project Result 1: Stop the motion on each of the four dates when the equation of time is zero and record the date and altitude of the Sun in the analemma table of the project report. After one complete year, make a printout of the Voyager screen. On the printout note the dates when the equation of time is zero and the corresponding altitudes of the Sun. Using a plus sign (+) or a minus sign (-) indicate on the printout where the equation of time is plus or minus.

Pulling the cursor from the **Forward** box stops the tracking and clicking in either the **Forward** or **Reverse** boxes resumes the motion. In order to more accurately determine the dates when the equation of time is zero you may want to decrease the time step to one day.

Project Result 2: Repeat the above for a different position, say, Detroit, Michigan. Make sure that all other Voyager settings are the same. Hand in a printout of the Sun's motion labeled as before.

Project Report 10

The Sun's Figure Eight

Name_____ Student Number_____

Project Goal:

PROJECT RESULTS

1. Analemma table, London/Greenwich

Latitude_____ Longitude_____

Standard time_____

Date (E = 0)	Altitude of Sun
_____	_____
_____	_____
_____	_____
_____	_____

Note: The standard time at Greenwich is the local mean time at 0 hours longitude, often written as GMT and called the Universal Time (UT).

A. Make a printout of the Voyager screen. On the printout note the dates when the equation of time is zero and the corresponding altitudes of the Sun.

B. Why is one part of the figure eight loop smaller than the other?

C. What causes the observed changes in the Sun's altitude?

D. Why is the figure eight centered on the meridian?

2. Analemma table, Detroit

Latitude_____   Date (E=0)_____Altitude of Sun
Longitude_____
Standard Time_____   _____

_____

_____

_____

NOTE: The standard time at Detroit is the local mean time of the Eastern Standard Time meridian at 5 hours west longitude.

A. Make a printout of the Voyager screen for this location. On the printout note the dates when the equation of time is zero and the corresponding altitudes of the Sun.

B. Why isn't the figure eight centered on the meridian at this new location?

Conclusions and Comments

PROJECT 11

The Fast Sidereal Clock

GOAL: TO INVESTIGATE THE GAIN IN LOCAL SIDEREAL TIME

SOLAR VERSUS SIDEREAL

The Sun moves eastward along the ecliptic by about 1 degree (4 minutes of time) per day. This apparent motion, caused by the Earth's revolution, causes stars to rise earlier each day. A star that rises with the Sun today will rise 4 minutes before the Sun tomorrow and 8 minutes before the Sun the next day. Likewise, a star that rises at 9 P.M. tonight will rise at 8:56 tomorrow and at 8:52 the next night.

The Earth's revolution also increases the time between two transits of the Sun, making the length of a solar day about 4 minutes longer than that of a sidereal day. A sidereal clock runs at a different rate than a clock keeping solar time. In fact, compared to a solar clock, a sidereal clock gains approximately 4 minutes each day.

Since a sidereal clock gains about 4 minutes each day, in 30 days it will gain 2 hours, and in 1 year it will gain 24 hours or 1 full day. It follows that there are 366 sidereal days in 365 solar days and that the length of a sidereal day is 365/366 the length of a solar day. This fraction implies that a sidereal day is 3 min 56 sec shorter than a solar day and that the actual daily gain of a sidereal clock is 3 min 56 sec rather than 4 minutes. Also, stars actually rise 3 min 56 sec earlier each day rather than 4 minutes earlier.

A sidereal clock's yearly gain of 1 full day suggests that once each year a sidereal clock must tell the same time as a solar clock. In fact solar and sidereal clocks show the same time at about midnight on the date of the autumnal equinox. The sidereal day is the actual time required for the Earth to rotate on its axis.

SET LOCATION AND TIME

You will once again be observing from London/Greenwich, England.

- ❑   Control@Set Location@Major Cities
- ❑   Select City@London
- ❑   Double Click or OK or Return
- ❑   Control@Set Time@Local Mean Time
- ❑   Dialog
  03/18/19??
  12:00 P.M.
  Daylight Savings Time No
- ❑   Double Click or OK or Return

GAINING ON TIME

To investigate how a sidereal clock gains time compared to a solar clock,

- ❑   Control Menu@ to SkyView@Local Horizon
- ❑   Scroll to South
- ❑   Display@Coordinate Lines@Meridian and
- ❑   Display@Coordinate Lines@Ecliptic

Project Result 1: Click on a star in the field of view and record its rising time in the Local Sidereal Time table of the project report. Repeat for each of the following six days using Control@Set Time@Local Mean Time to change the date. You should use the same star each day. Compute the daily gain in sidereal time.

Project Result 2: Repeat for six days starting on September 18. You will have to use a different star than you did before, but you should use the same star each day.

Project Report 11

The Fast Sidereal Clock

Name_____   Student Number_____

Project Goal:

PROJECT RESULTS

1. Local sidereal time table, March 18-23

Location: London, England   **Latitude:** $51^0\,30'$ **Longitude:** 0 hr
Universal Time _____ (A.M. or P.M.)   **Star**_____

Date	LST	Gain	Star Rising Time
March 18		0 min	
19			
20			
21			
22			
23			

Average gain   LST_____   **Gain rising** _____

2. Local sidereal time table, September 18-23

Location: London, England **Latitude:** $51^0 30'$ **Longitude:** 0 hr

Universal Time _____ (A.M. or P.M.) **Star**_____

Date	LST	Gain	Star Rising Time
Sep 18		0 min	
19			
20			
21			
22			
23			

Average gain LST_____ Gain rising _____

A. Stars rise about _____ minutes (earlier, later) each day.

B. On about what date are solar and sidereal time approximately the same? _____

C. The local sidereal day is (longer, shorter) than a solar day by about _____ minutes.

D. About how many sidereal days are there in one solar year? _____

E. Why are different constellations visible at different times of the year?

Conclusions and Comments

Chapter 7

Phases and Eclipses

Project 12   Waxing Eloquent

Lunar Phases

Project 13   Close Encounters

Conjunctions

Project 14   Shadowing the Moon

Lunar Eclipses

Project 15   Cover Up

Solar Eclipses

PROJECT 12

Waxing Eloquent

GOAL: TO OBSERVE THE PHASES OF THE MOON AND THE RELATIONSHIP BETWEEN PHASES AND THE POSITIONS OF THE SUN AND MOON

INTRODUCTION

Many centuries ago ancient astronomers recognized that the Moon goes through phases because it reflects sunlight as it revolves about the Earth. Pythagoras even argued that the Moon had to be a sphere, based on his observation that the region between illumination and darkness, the **terminator**, on the Moon's face was curved rather than a straight line.

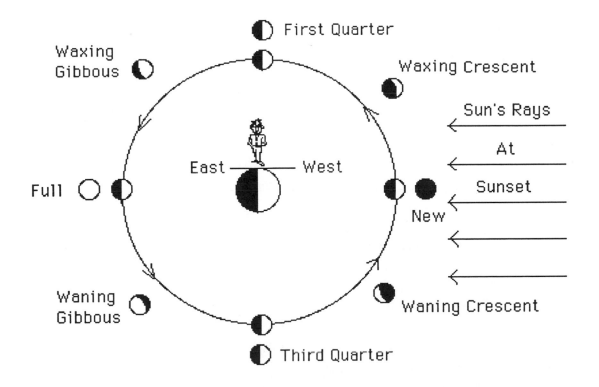

Figure 12.1   Lunar Phases

Figure 12.1 is drawn with the parallel rays of the distant Sun coming from the right. For an observer on the Earth the Sun is just setting. The outer circles indicate the observed positions and phases of the Moon around sunset through one cycle of phases. Notice that near new Moon the Moon sets around sunset while at full Moon the Moon rises at sunset. The inner circles show the Moon seen by an observer in space looking back at the Moon as it revolves about the Earth. Viewed from space the Moon does not go through phases and is always half illuminated, a so-called quarter phase.

The Moon's true period of revolution about the Earth is known as the **sidereal period** and is 27.3 days. The time between two new moons, called the **synodic period,** is 29.5 days.

SET LOCATION AND TIME

Pull down the **Control** menu to **Set Location** and use either **Major Cities** or **World Map** to specify the longitude and latitude of your location. For now, you need not worry about setting the date and time. Use the values that Voyager has entered.

LUNAR PHASES

In this activity you will watch the Moon as it goes through its phases.

- ❏   **Control@SkyView@Star Atlas**
- ❏   **Field@Center on Planet@Moon**
- ❏   **Options@Track Planets**
- ❏   **Objects Off**
- ❏   **Sun and Moon On**
- ❏   **Center Moon**
- ❏   **Lock Moon**
- ❏   **Time Step 1 hour**

Zoom in until the lunar disk is visible, click **Forward** and observe the Moon as it goes through its phases. When the Moon is near **new** phase pull the cursor from the **Forward** box to halt the motion and click on the Moon to bring up its **Information** box. If the information box does not indicate that the **Phase** is new, the **Age** is 0, and the **Illumination** is 0%, adjust the phase by clicking the **Reverse** or **Forward** boxes until these values are obtained.

Project Result 1: Complete the Lunar Phases table in the project report. Based on Figure 12.1 estimate the times that you would expect the new, first quarter, full, and third quarter moons to rise and set. Record your estimates in the Estimation table.

RISING AND SETTING TIMES

In order to more closely investigate the rising and setting times for various lunar phases,

- ❑ **Control@Set Time@Local Mean Time**
- ❑ **Dialog**
  Date of New Moon
  Sunset
  Daylight Savings Time No
- ❑ **Double Click or OK or Return**
- ❑ **Options@Track Planets**
- ❑ **Zoom Out**
- ❑ **Control@SkyView@Planetarium**
- ❑ **Scroll to Altitude 0 deg**
- ❑ **Center Moon**
- ❑ **Lock Moon**
- ❑ **Time Step to 1 day**

The Sun and Moon should be relatively close together in the western sky and both should be near the horizon.

Project Result 2: Forward the Moon through its phases, halting at those phases indicated in the Rising and Setting table of the project report. Record the requested information.

Suggested Procedure: The quickest way to forward through the phases might be,

- ❑ **Forward to Phase**
- ❑ **Click Moon**
- ❑ **Record Moon Information**
- ❑ **Center Sun**

❏   **Click Sun**
❏   **Record Sun Information**
❏   **Center Moon**
❏   **Lock Moon**
❏   **Forward to Phase**

ALONG THE ECLIPTIC

The observed phases of the Moon depend on the relative positions of the Sun and Moon as they both move eastward around the ecliptic. For example, when they are close together and have about the same right ascension the Moon's phase is new. In order to see the interplay between the relative positions and phases, reset the date to that of the new Moon and

❏   **Options@Track Planets**
❏   **Control@Sky View@Star Atlas**
❏   **Display@Coordinate Lines@Ecliptic**
❏   **Center Moon**
❏   **Lock Moon**
❏   **Forward to Phase**

Project Result 3: Use the previously suggested procedure to forward through the phases and complete the Relative Positions table in the project report.

Note: If you watch carefully you may see the Moon appear to wobble. This wobbly motion is due to the fact that you are observing from the Earth's surface! If you were looking from the Earth's center the Moon would not have this strange motion.

Optional Outside: Use Voyager to make star maps of the Moon's position and phases for a few evenings throughout a lunar cycle. Also note the Moon's rising and setting times as well as other data. Compare your printouts and data with the actual sky. Note any differences that you may observe. Keep an observing log showing sketches, sky conditions, time of observation, and estimated altitudes and azimuths of the Moon. Are any planets near the Moon? If so, check their positions on the star maps.

Project Report 12

Waxing Eloquent

Name_____ Student Number_____

Project Goal:

PROJECT RESULTS

1. Lunar phases table

Longitude_____(W or E) Latitude _____(N or S)

Date	Time	Phase	Age	Illumination	Magnitude
		New	0	0%	
		Waxing crescent			
		First quarter			
		Waxing gibbous			
		Full			
		Waning gibbous			
		Third quarter			
		Waning crescent			
		New			

Note: Magnitude relates to the brightness of the Moon. The smaller and more negative the magnitude number, the brighter the Moon.

A. Based on the information in the above table, what is the Moon's synodic period, that is, the time between two new

phases?_____ How does this compare with the
previously given value?

B. Estimation table, based on Figure 12.1

Phase	Rising time	Setting time
New		
First Quarter		
Full		
Third Quarter		
New		

Hint: For the times use sunset, noon, sunrise, or midnight

2. Rising and setting table

Sunset time_____

Longitude_____(W or E)   Latitude _____(N or S)

Date	Phase	Moon Rising	Moon Setting	Sun Rising	Sun Setting
	New				
	First quarter				
	Full				
	Third quarter				
	New				

A. Compare the above rising and setting times of the Moon with
your previous estimates. Note any differences.

B. The new moon rises about (sunrise, sunset) and sets about
(sunrise, sunset).

C. The full moon rises about (sunrise, sunset) and sets about
(sunrise, sunset).

D. As the Moon goes through its phases, it rises (earlier, later) each day.

3. Relative positions table

Longitude_____(W or E)   Latitude _____(N or S)

Date	Phase	Moon R.A.	Dec.	Sun R.A.	Dec.
_____	New				
_____	First quarter				
_____	Full				
_____	Third quarter				
_____	New				

A. What is the difference between the right ascensions of the Sun and Moon when the phase of the Moon is

(1) New _____

(2) First quarter _____

(3) Full _____

(4) Third quarter _____

B. About how many degrees does the Moon move eastward each day?_____

C. Does the Moon move exactly along the ecliptic?_____
Explain why.

Conclusions and Comments

PROJECT 13

Close Encounters

GOAL: TO LEARN ABOUT CONJUNCTIONS AND OCCULTATIONS

INTRODUCTION

If the angular separation between two celestial objects is small and they therefore appear close together in the sky they are said to be in **conjunction.** For example, two planets, a planet and a star, or the Sun and Moon can be in conjunction. In the latter case the phase of the Moon will be new and an eclipse of the Sun is possible. As the Sun, Moon, and planets move around the zodiac they often come between us and a more distant object. An **occultation** is when a closer and apparently larger object, such as the Moon, covers up a smaller more distant object such as a star or planet.

Figure 13.1 Conjunction Search

Voyager allows you to predict conjunctions, occultations, and related phenomena such as new and full Moons, and lunar and solar eclipses. In this project you will learn how to use this powerful tool (see Figure 13.1).

SET LOCATION AND TIME

Pull down the **Control** menu to **Set Location** and use either **Major Cities** or **World Map** to set the longitude and latitude of your location. For now, you need not worry about setting the date and time. Use the values that Voyager has entered.

SEARCHING FOR NEW AND FULL MOONS

A **new Moon** can be found by looking for conjunctions between the Sun and Moon. A **full Moon** occurs when there is a conjunction between the Moon and the Earth's shadow.

- ❑   **Control@SkyView@Star Atlas**
- ❑   **Display@Major Planets@Earth-Moon Shadow**
- ❑   **Options@Track Planets**
- ❑   **Time Step 1 hour**
- ❑   **Options@Conjunction Search**
- ❑   **Dialog**
        Select Sun and Moon
        Search From This Year
        Search To Next Year
        Separation 7 deg
- ❑   **Click Search**

As the search proceeds, the date, time, and angular separation of each conjunction are displayed. An asterisk (*) next to a conjunction indicates that one or both objects are below the horizon at your location when the conjunction takes place. If you wish to stop the search before it is completed you can click the **Stop** button. Double click on the listed conjunction to display the sky with the objects centered on the screen. You can also highlight the listed conjunction and click the **Set Time** button.

When your search is completed look at a few of the conjunctions and use **Forward** and **Reverse** to watch the motion of the Moon near new and full phase.

Project Result 1:   Hand in a printout of the dates of new Moons along with a printout of a Sun-new Moon conjunction. Before you make a printout turn the sky white. Note that since you are using a white sky the new Moon will appear white and the Sun and full Moon will appear black!

Project Result 2:   Select the Moon and the Earth's shadow and repeat the above conjunction search. Hand in a printout of the dates of full Moons along with a printout of a full Moon-Earth shadow conjunction.

AN OCCULTATION OF VENUS

Find the date of the Moon's occultation of Venus in 1993 using **Conjunction Search** with the separation set for 0.1 degrees. View the occultation using **Forward** and **Reverse**.

Project Result 3:   Hand in a printout of this event.

Project Report 13

Close Encounters

Name_____   Student Number_____

Project Goal:

PROJECT RESULTS

1. Printouts of the dates of new Moons along with a printout of a Sun-Moon conjunction

2. Printouts of the dates of full Moons along with a printout of a full Moon-Earth shadow conjunction

    A. Why does the Moon usually pass either above or below the Sun and the Earth's shadow when it is in a new and full phase?

3. Printout of Moon-Venus occultation

Longitude_____(W or E)   Latitude _____(N or S)

Date_____   Time_____

    A. Was the occultation visible from your location?_____

Conclusions and Comments

PROJECT 14

Shadowing the Moon

GOAL: TO LEARN ABOUT LUNAR ECLIPSES

LUNAR ECLIPSE CONDITIONS

As the Moon revolves about the Earth it sometimes passes through the Earth's shadow. When this happens a lunar eclipse occurs. As you can see from Figure 14.1, a necessary condition for a lunar eclipse is that the Moon be in a full phase. But although the Moon goes through the full phase once each month there is not an eclipse each month. This implies that the full Moon does not usually pass through the shadow. Generally, the Moon passes either above or below the shadow. Hence, the Moon being in a full phase is a necessary but not a sufficient condition for an eclipse.

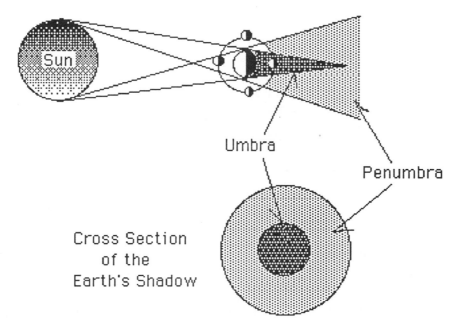

Figure 14.1   Lunar Eclipse Geometry

The other required condition is, of course, that the Moon must pass through the shadow, which can happen only if the Moon is in or close to the Earth's orbital plane. This plane, called the ecliptic, derives its name from the requirement that the Moon be near the plane for an eclipse to occur. The reason that the Moon is not always in the ecliptic is that the Moon's orbital plane is inclined to the ecliptic plane by about five degrees.

The Earth's shadow has two parts. The inner, darker region is called the **umbra** and the outer, lighter region is called the **penumbra**. Neither the umbra nor the penumbra is completely dark because the Earth's atmosphere scatters sunlight into the shadow. During an eclipse the Moon darkens and becomes redder, but does not completely disappear.

Figure 14.2 indicates the possible types of lunar eclipses. When the Moon is in the penumbra, only a very small darkening occurs, so penumbral eclipses are difficult to detect with the naked eye. It is partial and total umbral eclipses that are most easily seen.

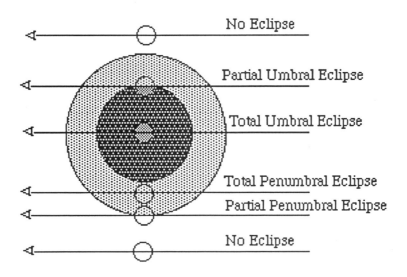

Figure 14.2   Types of Lunar Eclipses

SET LOCATION AND TIME

Pull down the **Control Menu** to **Set Location** and use either **Major Cities** or **World Map** to set the longitude and latitude of your

location. For now, you need not worry about setting the date and time.
Use the values that Voyager has entered.

PREDICTING LUNAR ECLIPSES

To determine the dates and times of lunar eclipses you will search
for conjunctions between the Moon and the Earth's shadow.

❑   **Control@Sky View@Star Atlas**
❑   **Display@Major Planets@Earth-Moon Shadow On**
❑   **Options@Track Planets**
❑   **Time Step 1 hour**
❑   **Options@Conjunction Search**
❑   **Dialog**
      Select Moon and Earth's Shadow
      Search From This Year
      Search To Next Year
      Separation 0.4 deg
❑   **Click Search**

As the search proceeds the date and time of each possible eclipse
are displayed. An asterisk (*) next to a date indicates that the Moon
may be below your horizon. If this is the case all or some of the eclipse
will not be visible from your location. If you wish to stop the search
before it is completed you can click the **Stop** button. Double click on
the listed conjunction to display the sky with the objects centered on the
screen. You can also highlight the listed conjunction and click the **Set
Time** button. **Zoom in** until you can clearly see the Earth's shadow
and the Moon's disk.

When your search is completed look at each of the possible
eclipse dates and use **Forward** and **Reverse** to watch the motion of the
Moon. You may want to use a smaller time step. To choose the next
listed eclipse date simply go back to the conjunction search dialog box
by selecting **Conjunction Search** from the **Options** menu. If your
search did not find any total or partial umbral eclipses it might be that
there were none in the specified time interval. Try a different, or
perhaps longer, time interval. It might also be that the separation angle
was not small enough. Try setting the separation angle somewhere
between 0 and 0.4 and redo the search.

Project Result 1:   Hand in a printout showing a total or partial umbral eclipse and answer the related questions. Before you make a printout turn the sky white. Note that since you are using a white sky the full Moon will appear black and the eclipsed Moon will appear white!

Project Result 2: The type and visibility of an eclipse may be different at different locations on the Earth. Use the same eclipse date and time that you identified in the above result but choose a location having a different latitude and longitude. Hand in a printout showing the eclipse and answer the related questions.

Project Result 3: Search for eclipses over a time interval of six or more years. What is the average yearly frequency of all types of lunar eclipses?

Project Report 14

Shadowing the Moon

Name_____   Student Number_____

Project Goal:

PROJECT RESULTS

1. Printout showing a total or partial umbral lunar eclipse

    A. Eclipse data

        Longitude_____(W, E) Latitude _____(N, S)

        Date_____   Time_____

        Lunar rising time_____

        Lunar setting time_____

        Type of lunar eclipse_____

    B. At this location (all, part, none) of the eclipse was visible.

    C. About how long was part or all of the Moon in the Earth's shadow regions?_____ If the eclipse was total, determine the duration of totality, that is, the time that the Moon was totally within the umbra. _____

D. Recalling that the apparent size of the Moon is one-half a degree, estimate the diameter of the umbra and penumbra in degrees.

    (1) Angular size of umbra_____

    (2) Angular size of penumbra_____

E. The Moon moves eastward about one-half a degree per hour. If the Moon passed directly through the center of the Earth's shadow how long would the Moon remain completely in the umbra? In the penumbra?

    (1) Time in umbra_____

    (2) Time in penumbra_____

2. Printout showing eclipse at new location.

A. Eclipse data

    Longitude_____(W, E)   Latitude _____(N, S)

    Date_____   Time_____

    Lunar rising time_____

    Lunar setting time_____

    Type of lunar eclipse_____

B. At this location (all, part, none) of the eclipse was visible.

C. About how long was part or all of the Moon in the Earth's shadow regions?_____ If the eclipse was total, determine the duration of totality, that is, the time that the Moon was totally within the umbra. _____

    D. Estimated diameter of the umbra and penumbra in degrees.

        (1) Angular size of umbra_____

        (2) Angular size of penumbra_____

3. Lunar eclipse frequency

    A. Time interval of search_____

    B. Separation angle_____

    C. Average yearly frequency of eclipses_____

Conclusions and Comments

PROJECT 15

Cover Up

GOAL: TO LEARN ABOUT SOLAR ECLIPSES

SOLAR ECLIPSE CONDITIONS

As the Moon revolves about the Earth it sometimes passes between the Earth and the Sun. When this happens a solar eclipse results. As you can see from the Figure 15.1, a necessary condition for a solar eclipse is that the Moon be in a new phase. But although the Moon goes through the new phase once each month there is not an eclipse each month. This implies that the Moon does not usually pass directly between the Earth and Sun at new moon.

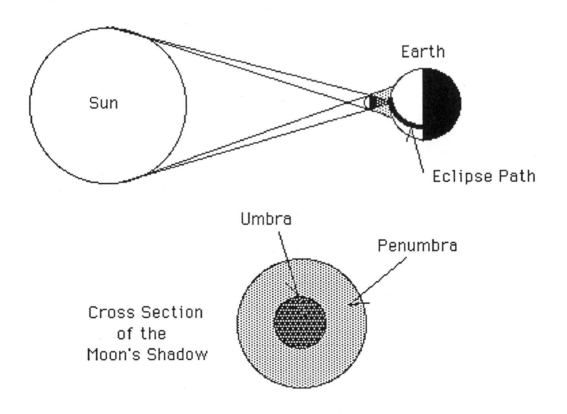

Figure 15.1   Solar Eclipse Geometry

Generally, the Moon passes either above or below the Sun. Hence, the Moon being in a new phase is a necessary but not a sufficient condition for an eclipse. The other required condition for a solar eclipse is that the Moon must pass directly between the Earth and Sun, which can happen only if the Moon is in the ecliptic plane. The reason that the Moon is not always in the ecliptic is that the Moon's orbital plane is inclined to the ecliptic plane by about five degrees.

Just as the Earth's shadow has two parts, so does the shadow of the Moon. The inner, darker region is called the **umbra** and the outer, lighter region is called the **penumbra**.

Figure 15.2 shows the possible types and duration of solar eclipses. Notice that the Moon's shadow covers a relatively small area on the Earth's surface. Only those few people who are in the shadow region will actually see an eclipse. Individuals in the penumbra will see a partial eclipse while those in the umbra will view a total eclipse. The Moon's shadow sweeps across the Earth's surface from west to east, and an eclipse is seen at different times by people at different locations. The path travelled by the Moon's umbra is known as the **eclipse path.**

A. Longest Duration   B. Shortest Duration

C. Annular Eclipse

Figure 15.2   Eclipse Types and Duration

Because the Moon revolves about the Earth in an elliptical orbit its distance from the Earth varies. When the Moon is close to the Earth its apparent size is larger than when it is far from the Earth. If an eclipse occurs when the Moon is close, its apparent size will be somewhat larger than that of the Sun, the eclipse path will be wider, and the duration of the eclipse will be longer (Figure 15.2, A). The maximum possible duration of totality is around eight minutes. The reverse is true when the Moon is far from the Earth (Figure 15.2, B). From time to time the Moon can be so far away that its apparent size is less than the Sun's. When this happens the Moon does not completely cover up the Sun, and a ring (annulus) of sunlight remains visible around the Moon. This type of eclipse is called an **annular eclipse** (Figure 15.2, C).

The outermost part of the Sun's atmosphere, the **corona**, is a very faint, tenuous gas that is difficult to observe with ground-based telescopes except during a total solar eclipse. For this reason astronomers have historically gone to great lengths and great distances to observe solar eclipses. Now that orbiting instruments have made it possible to produce artificial eclipses with some ease the scientific importance of natural eclipses is not quite as great. However, the esthetic aspects of solar eclipses still make them one of the most striking and exciting of astronomical events.

SET LOCATION AND TIME

Pull down the **Control Menu** to **Set Location** and use either **Major Cities** or **World Map** to set the longitude and latitude of your location. For now, you need not worry about setting the date and time.

PREDICTING SOLAR ECLIPSES

To determine the dates and times of solar eclipses you will search for conjunctions between the Moon and Sun.

- ❑ **Control@SkyView@Star Atlas**
- ❑ **Display@Major Planets@Earth-Moon Shadow**
- ❑ **Options@Track Planets**
- ❑ **Time Step 1 hour**
- ❑ **Options@Conjunction Search**
- ❑ **Dialog**
  Select Moon and Sun
  Search From This Year
  Search To Next Year
  Separation 0.4 deg
- ❑ **Click Search**

As the search proceeds, the date and time of each possible eclipse is displayed. An asterisk (*) next to a date indicates that the Moon may be below your horizon. If this is the case all or some of the eclipse will not be visible from your location. If you wish to stop the search before it is completed you can click the **Stop** button. Double click on the listed conjunction to display the sky with the objects centered on the screen. You can also highlight the listed conjunction and click the **Set Time** button. **Zoom in** until you can clearly see the disks of the Sun and the Moon.

When your search is completed look at each of the possible eclipse dates and use **Forward** and **Reverse** to watch the motion of the Moon. You may want to use a smaller time step. To choose the next listed eclipse date simply go back to the conjunction search dialog box by selecting **Conjunction Search** from the **Options** menu. If your search did not find any total or partial solar eclipses it might be that there were none in the specified time interval. Try a different, or perhaps longer, time interval. It might also be that the separation angle was not small enough. Try setting the separation angle somewhere between 0 and 0.4 and redo the search.

Project Result 1:   Hand in a printout showing a total or partial solar eclipse and answer the related questions. Before you make a printout turn the sky white. Note that since you are using a white sky the new Moon will appear white and the Sun will appear black!

Project Result 2: Search for eclipses over a time interval of six or more years. What is the average yearly frequency of all types of solar eclipses?

THE SOLAR ECLIPSE OF JULY 1991

A relatively long solar eclipse visible from the northern hemisphere took place on July 1991. To view this eclipse from Honolulu,

- ❑   **Control@Sky View@Local Horizon**
- ❑   **Control@Set Location@Major Cities**
- ❑   **Select City@Honolulu**
- ❑   **Control@Set Time@Local Mean Time**
- ❑   **Dialog**
      July 11, 1991

6:00 A.M.
Daylight Savings Time No
- [ ] OK or Return
- [ ] Options@Track Planets
- [ ] Objects Off
- [ ] Sun and Moon On
- [ ] Center Sun
- [ ] Lock Sun
- [ ] Time Step 10 minutes
- [ ] Forward

Project Result 3: Hand in a white sky printout showing the solar eclipse and answer the related questions.

Project Result 4: The type and visibility of an eclipse may be different at different locations on the Earth. Repeat for La Paz, Mexico.

FROM THE MOON'S POINT OF VIEW

With Voyager you can view a solar eclipse from the Moon and see the eclipse path as the Moon's umbral shadow sweeps across the Earth's surface.

- [ ] Display@Major Planets@Planet Images
- [ ] Dialog
  Earth Disk On
- [ ] OK or Return
- [ ] Control@SkyView@Solar System
- [ ] Options@Observe From Planet@Moon
- [ ] Control@Set Time@Universal Time
- [ ] Dialog
  July 11, 1991
  17:00
- [ ] OK or Return
- [ ] Options@Track Planets
- [ ] Objects Off
- [ ] Earth On
- [ ] Center Earth
- [ ] Lock Earth
- [ ] Display@Hide Stars
- [ ] Time Step 10 minutes

❑ **Display@Major Planets@Earth-Moon Shadow On**
❑ **Zoom in till Continents Visible**
❑ **Forward**

Project Result 5: Turn the sky white and make a printout of the Moon's shadow on the Earth. Sketch the direction of motion of the Moon's shadow and note the approximate times that the shadow crosses Honolulu and La Paz.

Project Report 15

Cover Up

Name_____   Student Number_____

Project Goal:

PROJECT RESULTS

1.   Printout showing a total or partial solar eclipse

    A. Eclipse data

        Longitude_____(W, E)   Latitude _____(N, S)

        Date_____   Time_____

        Lunar rising time_____

        Lunar setting time_____

        Type of solar eclipse_____

    B. At this location (all, part, none) of the eclipse was visible.

    C. About how long did the eclipse last?_____ If the eclipse was total, estimate the duration of totality, that is, the time that the Sun was totally covered by the Moon. _____

2. Solar eclipse frequency

   A. Time interval of search_____

   B. Separation angle_____

   C. Average yearly frequency of eclipses_____

3. Printout showing July 1991 solar eclipse, Honolulu, Hawaii

   A. Eclipse location and type

   Latitude _____   Longitude _____

   Date_____   Time_____

   Type of solar eclipse_____

   Beginning _____

   Middle _____

   Ending _____

   B. At this location (all, part, none) of the eclipse was visible.

   C. About how long did the eclipse last?_____ If the
   eclipse was total, estimate the duration of totality, that is, the time
   that the Sun was totally covered by the Moon.

   _____

4. Printout showing July 1991 solar eclipse, La Paz, Mexico

   A. Eclipse location and type

   Latitude _____   longitude _____

   Date_____   Time_____

   Type of solar eclipse_____

Beginning _____

Middle _____

Ending _____

B. At this location (all, part, none) of the eclipse was visible.

C. About how long did the eclipse last?_____ If the eclipse was total, estimate the duration of totality, that is, the time that the Sun was totally covered by the Moon.

_____

D. What differences did you observe between Honolulu and La Paz?

5.   Printout of July 1991 eclipse seen from Moon

A.   Phase of Earth _____

B.   Direction of motion of the Moon's shadow _____

C.   Time that shadow crosses

Honolulu _____

La Paz _____

Conclusions and Comments

Chapter 8

Planetary Phases and Motions

PROJECT 16

Aspects

GOAL: TO LEARN ABOUT THE PHASES AND PERIODS OF PLANETS

INFERIOR AND SUPERIOR PLANETS

The planets Mercury and Venus, closer to the Sun than the Earth, are called the **inferior planets** while planets farther from the Sun than the Earth are termed the **superior planets** (Mars, Jupiter, etc.). Viewed from the Earth, all planets go through phases as they revolve about the Sun. However, the inferior planets exhibit different phases than the superior planets.   Inferior planets go through the same phases as the Moon (Figure 16.1), but the superior planets show only two phases (Figures 16.2), namely, full and gibbous.

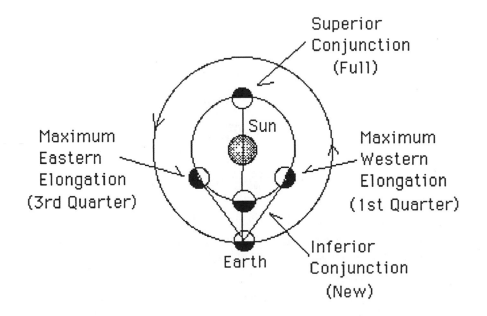

Figure 16.1   Inferior Planet Phases

When an inferior planet is between the Earth and the Sun its phase is new and it is said to be at **inferior conjunction**. As it moves about the Sun, the planet's phase and the angle between it and the Sun both change. The angle, called the **angle of elongation**, varies from 0 degrees at inferior conjunction (new) to a maximum value at **maximum western elongation** (first quarter), to 0 degrees at **superior conjunction** (full), to another maximum value at **maximum eastern elongation** (third quarter), and finally back to 0 degrees at inferior conjunction. The maximum angles of elongation, either east or west, are about 28 degrees for Mercury and 48 degrees for Venus. So these planets are never seen very far from the Sun.

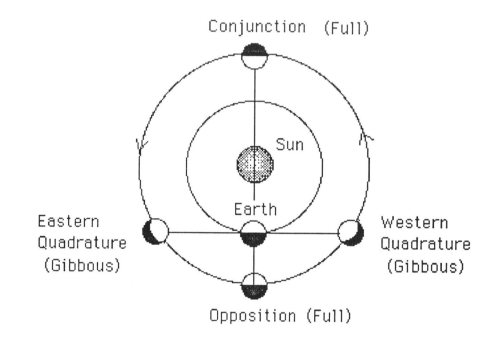

Figure 16.2 Superior Planet Phases

Looking south, a planet at eastern elongation would be to the left of the Sun while at western elongation it would appear to the right of the Sun. An inferior planet east (left) of the Sun rises after the Sun and sets after the Sun. Since it is visible in the evening sky around sunset it is sometimes referred to as an **evening "star."** If the planet is west (right) of the Sun it rises before the Sun and being visible in the morning is often called a **morning "star."**

Usually planets move eastward through the zodiac, but from time to time they change their direction of motion and move westward. This westward motion is known as **retrograde motion**. Inferior planets retrograde near inferior conjunction.

The phase of a superior planet changes from full when the planet is at **opposition**, to gibbous at **western quadrature**, to full at **conjunction**, to gibbous at **eastern quadrature**, and back to full at opposition. A superior planet retrogrades when it is near opposition.

Copernicus pointed out in the fifteenth century that one can define two periods of revolution for each planet. The actual period he called the **sidereal period**, the other he referred to as the **synodic period**. This latter period is what can be observed from the Earth and it is affected by the Earth's motion as well as the planet's motion. For an inferior planet the synodic period can be defined as the time between two inferior conjunctions and for a superior planet, as the time between two oppositions.

SET LOCATION AND TIME

Pull down the **Control Menu** to **Set Location** and use either **Major Cities** or **World Map** to set the longitude and latitude of your location. For now, you need not worry about setting the date and time. Use the values that Voyager has entered.

THE ORRERY

The orrery was originally a mechanical device that could be used to demonstrate the relative positions and motions of the planets. The Voyager equivalent, minus the gears and pulleys, can be found under the **Options** menu. Figure 16.3 shows the orrery screen. In this screen you are looking down on the solar system. Your distance from the Sun can be selected by clicking the up/down arrows next to the **Field Diameter** box. The date shown is the date that has been set when you started Voyager. Clicking the up/down arrows next to the **Date** box will cause the planets to move forward or backward in time. Note that the date corresponds to a Universal Time which is the Greenwich Mean time, not your local time. Printouts of the orrery screen can be made by choosing **Print Orrery** under the **File** menu.

Project Result 1: Hand in an orrery printout showing Venus at inferior conjunction and a second printout showing Mars at opposition. Also note the times when Venus is at superior conjunction and Mars is at conjunction.

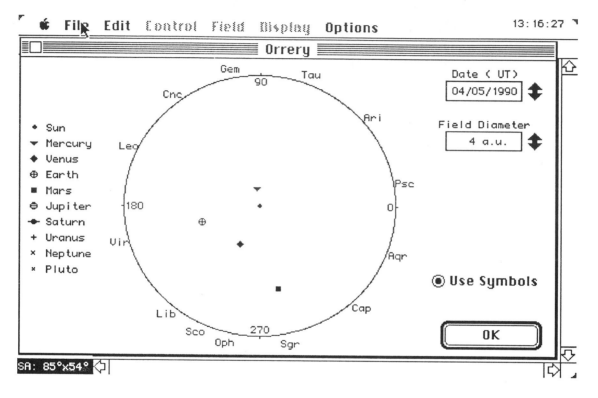

Figure 16.3   The Orrery Screen

FOLLOWING THE PHASES

Viewed from the Earth the planets go through phases as they revolve about the Sun. With the aid of Voyager you can observe these phases without a telescope.

❑   Display@Major Planets@Planet Images
     Dialog
     Venus Disk On
     Mars Disk On
❑   **OK or Return**
❑   **Control Menu@SkyView@Star Atlas**
❑   **Control@Set Time@Universal Time**
❑   **Dialog**
     Venus Inferior Conjunction Date

18:00
❑   OK or Return
❑   Options@Track Planets
❑   Objects Off
❑   Sun and Venus On
❑   Center Venus
❑   Lock Venus
❑   Zoom in to Venus Disk
❑   Time Step 2 days
❑   Forward
❑   Halt at Phase
❑   Click Venus for Info
❑   Forward

Project Result 2: Record your data in the Venus Phase table of the project report. You can more accurately determine the phases by using the **% illumination** in the **Information** box. Use **Forward** and **Reverse** with perhaps a change in step size to more closely determine the illumination corresponding to the desired phase.

Project Result 3: Repeat for Mars with the date set for opposition and the time step set at about 1 week.

Project Report 16

Aspects

Name_____   **Student Number**_____

Project Goal:

PROJECT RESULTS

1. Printouts showing Venus at inferior conjunction and Mars at opposition

   A. Venus

   Date of inferior conjunction _____ Phase_____

   Date of superior conjunction _____ Phase _____

   B. Mars

   Date of opposition _____ Phase _____

   Date of conjunction _____ Phase _____

   C. Can Venus be seen when it is at superior conjunction?_____   Explain your answer.

   D. Can Mars be seen when it is at conjunction?_____ Explain your answer.

   E. At opposition Mars should rise at about (sunrise, sunset).

2. Venus phase table

Date	Phase (Illum.)	Apparent Mag.	Size	Earth Dist.	Times Rising	Setting
	New (0%)					
	First quarter (50%)					
	Full (100%)					
	Third quarter (50%)					
	New (0%)					

3. Mars phase table

Date	Phase (Illum.)	Apparent Mag.	Size	Earth Dist.	Times Rising	Setting
	Full (100%)					
	Gibbous (90%)					
	Full (100%)					
	Gibbous (90%)					
	Full (100%)					

A. From your data and the definition of synodic periods estimate

    (1) The synodic period of Venus _____

    (2) The synodic period of Mars _____

B. Explain why the apparent sizes and magnitudes of the planets change as Venus and Mars go through their phases.

Conclusions and Comments

PROJECT 17

The Morning and Evening Stars

GOAL: TO LEARN ABOUT THE RISING AND SETTING TIMES OF INFERIOR AND SUPERIOR PLANETS

INTRODUCTION

Recall that **inferior** planets (Figure 17.1) go through the same phases as the Moon but that the **superior** planets (Figure 17.2) have only two phases, namely, full and gibbous.

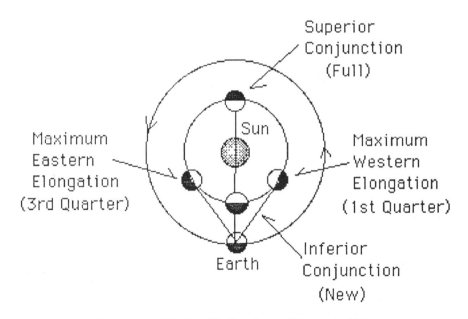

Figure 17.1   Inferior Planet Phases

Looking south, a planet at eastern elongation would be to the left of the Sun while at western elongation it would appear to the right of the Sun. An inferior planet east (left) of the Sun rises after the Sun and sets after the Sun. Since it is visible in the evening sky around sunset it is sometimes referred to as an **evening "star."** If the planet is west (right) of the Sun it rises before the Sun and being visible in the morning is often called a **morning "star."**

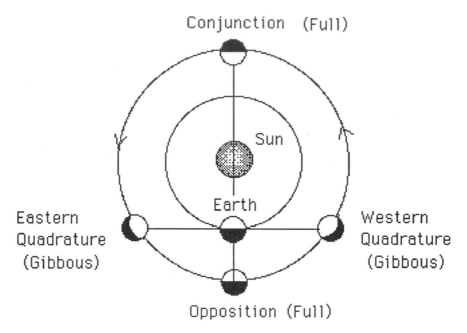

Figure 17.2   Superior Planet Phases

SET LOCATION AND TIME

Pull down the **Control Menu** to **Set Location** and use either **Major Cities** or **World Map** to set the longitude and latitude of your location. For now, you need not worry about setting the date and time. Use the values that Voyager has entered.

ELONGATION AND OPPOSITION

Select **Orrery** from the **Options** menu. Your distance from the Sun can be selected by clicking the up/down arrows next to the **Field Diameter** box. The date shown is the date that has been set when you started Voyager. Clicking the up/down arrows next to the **Date** box will cause the planets to move forward or backward in time. Printouts of the orrery screen can be made by choosing **Print Orrery** under the **File** menu.

Project Result 1: Use the orrery to find the approximate dates of maximum **western** elongation for Mercury, maximum **eastern** elongation for Venus, and the date of **opposition** for Mars. Record these dates in the project report. Also record the rising and setting times of the Sun and planets.

EAST AND WEST OF THE SUN

With Voyager you can watch the rising and setting of the Sun and planets.

- ❑   **Control@SkyView@Local Horizon.**
- ❑   **Display@White Sky**
- ❑   **Control@Set Time@Local Mean Time**
- ❑   **Dialog**
      Mercury Maximum Western Elongation Date
      Rising Time
- ❑   **OK or Return**
- ❑   **Field@Center on Planet@Mercury**
- ❑   **File@Print Sky Chart**

Use **Angular Separation** in the **Field** menu to measure the angular separation between Mercury and the Sun.

- ❑   **Click Mercury**
- ❑   **Click Sun**
- ❑   **Field@Angular Separation**

Project Result 2: Hand in three printouts showing the **rising** of Mercury and Mars and the **setting** of Venus. Record the angular separation between the planet and the Sun.

Project Report 17

The Morning and Evening Stars

Name_____ Student Number_____

Project Goal:

PROJECT RESULTS

1. Elongation and opposition

A. Mercury western elongation data

Western elongation date _____
Planetrise _____ Planetset _____
Sunrise _____ Sunset _____

B. Venus eastern elongation data

Eastern elongation date _____
Planetrise _____ Planetset _____
Sunrise _____ Sunset _____

C. Mars opposition data

Opposition date _____
Planetrise _____ Planetset _____
Sunrise _____ Sunset _____

2. Three printouts showing the rising of Mercury and Mars and the setting of Venus

    A. Angular separation between the Sun and

        (1) Mercury at maximum western elongation_____

        (2) Venus at maximum eastern elongation_____

        (3) Mars at opposition_____

    B. At western elongation Mercury rises (before, after) the Sun and is a (morning, evening) object.

    C. At eastern elongation Venus rises (before, after) the Sun and is a (morning, evening) object.

    D. At opposition Mars is to the (west, east) of the Sun and rises about (sunset, sunrise).

Conclusions and Comments

PROJECT 18

Backing It Up

GOAL: TO LEARN ABOUT THE RETROGRADE MOTION OF PLANETS

RETROGRADE MOTION

In previous projects you have learned about planetary phases. Recall that Mercury and Venus, the **inferior planets**, go through the same phases as the Moon while the **superior planets** such as Mars exhibit only the full and gibbous phase.

Although the ancient astronomers could not see the phases of the planets they closely followed their changing positions. By the time of the Babylonians it was known that planets do not always move eastward through the zodiac but from time to time back up and move westward. This westward motion is called **retrograde motion.** Inferior planets retrograde around **inferior conjunction** (Figure 16.1) while superior planets retrograde near **opposition** (Figure 16.2).

THE GEOCENTRIC THEORY

Ancient astronomers were able to account for not only retrograde motion but the related fact that planets seemed brightest when they were retrograding. One early explanation was suggested by the Alexandrian mathematician **Apollonius** and later refined by the great Greek astronomer, **Claudius Ptolemy.** The **Ptolemaic theory** was very flexible and consequently quite complex.

Like most early theories, Ptolemy's was a geocentric theory. Since the Earth neither rotated nor revolved, all planetary motions were explained as real motions about the Earth. Each planet moved around a small circle called an **epicycle** as the center of the epicycle revolved around a larger circle, the **deferent**, centered on the Earth. This combination of circular motions caused a planet to move in a path such as that shown in Figure 18.1.

Notice that usually the planet is moving eastward around the Earth but from time to time its direction of motion reverses and it moves westward. Also, when it is retrograding it is closest to the Earth and is therefore brightest.

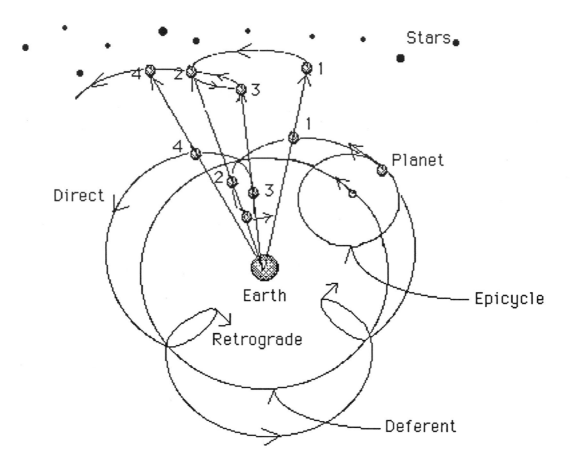

Figure 18.1   Retrograde Motion in the Ptolemaic System

This brilliant theory survived for centuries and through the centuries it was revised and made ever more complex. Although it seemed to explain all of the observed planetary motions it was, of course, incorrect. The Earth is not at the center of the solar system and there are no epicycles and deferents.

THE HELIOCENTRIC THEORY

The Ptolemaic system was eventually replaced by a simpler and more accurate explanation, the **heliocentric theory**. One of the first advocates of this theory was the Greek astronomer **Aristarchus**. It was not, however, until **Copernicus** revived this idea in the fifteenth century that it began to receive the attention it deserved. But the first accurate statement of how planets actually move was made by the German astronomer **Johannes Kepler**. Between 1609 and 1618 Kepler, using the observations of the Danish astronomer **Tycho Brahe**, discovered three laws that describe planetary motions (see Chapter 1).

In the modern heliocentric theory the planets revolve around the Sun in elliptical orbits with periods of revolution that increase with increasing distance from the Sun. Mercury takes only 88 days to move about the Sun while the most distant planet, Pluto, takes some 247 years. It is this relationship between period and distance that results in the retrograde motion of planets (Figure 18.2).

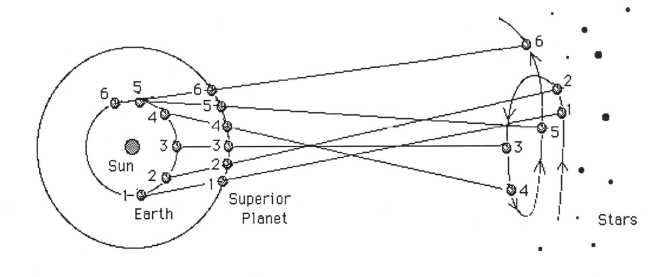

Figure 18.2 Retrograde Motion in the Heliocentric Theory

Because the Earth moves faster than any of the superior planets it overtakes and passes these planets at regular intervals. This happens when the planet is at **opposition** (position 3 in Figure 18.2). At opposition the Earth and planet are relatively close together and the planet, therefore, appears brighter than at any other time. As the Earth passes the planet, the planet seems to back up, just as a car that you speed by on an expressway seems momentarily to be going backwards. Thus, superior planets retrograde and appear brightest when they are near opposition. At this time they are also in a full phase and would rise about sunset. This happens every 2.1 years for Mars and about every year for the other superior planets.

The time between oppositions is known as the **synodic period**. The synodic period of Mars is 779.9 days or 2.1 years, but for more distant planets the synodic period decreases, approaching 1 year for the most distant planets. Jupiter, for example, is at opposition every 398.9 days while Pluto is at opposition every 366.7 days.

Mercury and Venus, the inferior planets, also retrograde and vary in brightness. However, for these two planets the retrograde motion occurs when they overtake and pass the slower moving Earth near **inferior conjunction.** The synodic period for the inferior planets is defined as the time between two inferior conjunctions. For Mercury this period is 115.9 days and for Venus it is 584.0 days.

SET LOCATION AND TIME

Pull down the **Control** menu to **Set Location** and use either **Major Cities** or **World Map** to indicate your location. Then,

- ❑   **Control@Set Time@Local Mean Time**
- ❑   **Dialog**
       08/11/1990
       5:00 P.M.
       Daylight Savings Time No
- ❑   **Double Click or OK or Return**

THE RETROGRADE MOTION OF MARS

With the aid of Voyager you are going to observe the retrograde motion of the superior planet Mars.

- ❑   **Control@Sky View@Star Atlas**
- ❑   **Display@White Sky**

❑   **Options@Track Planets**
❑   **Objects Off**
❑   **Mars On**
❑   **Center Mars**
❑   **Lock Mars**
❑   **Path On**
❑   **Time Step 1 week**
❑   **Forward**

Project Result 1: Starting on 08/11/1990 view the complete retrograde motion of Mars and make a printout of this motion. You might also find it instructive to view the same time interval using the **Orrery** in the **Options** menu.

Project Result 2: Reset the date to 08/11/1990. Click on Mars to bring up its information box. Record the information requested in the Mars Retrograde Motion 1990 table of the project report and use **Forward** or **Set Time** to advance Mars' position to the next date in the table.

Astronomers frequently express the apparent brightness of an object using numbers called **apparent magnitudes**. The magnitudes for observable celestial objects, from the Sun to the farthest galaxies, range from about -27 to about +27. Each difference of one magnitude corresponds to a brightness factor of 2.512, and the smaller or more negative the magnitude the brighter the object. Hence, a first magnitude object is 2.512 times brighter than a second magnitude object, but a first magnitude object is 2.512 x 2.512 or 2.512^2 times brighter than an object of third magnitude. The apparent brightness of the Sun is some 2.512^{54} times greater than the brightness of the faintest galaxies. This is truly an astronomically large number!

As the distance between the Earth and Mars changes, the apparent brightness and angular size of Mars also change. The **Planet Magnitudes** command plots the changing magnitude (small dots) and angular size (large dots) of a planet as viewed from the Earth. The buttons at the bottom of the screen allow you to plot this data for each of the three listed years. The **Print Magnitudes** command will print the displayed graph.

❑   **Options@Planet Magnitudes**

❑ **Click Year Button**
❑ **Click Mars Box**
❑ **File@Print Magnitudes**

Project Result 3:   Make a printout of the **Planet Magnitudes** screen for the year(s) that Mars retrogrades and discuss the reason for the observed changes in brightness and angular size. It is very important to remember that the smaller the magnitude the brighter the object.

Project Result 4:   Make a printout showing Mars' retrograde motion at its next opposition. Remember that the synodic period of Mars is 2.1 years.

THE RETROGRADE MOTION OF VENUS

The inferior planets Mercury and Venus also retrograde. Use the **Orrery** to determine the approximate date when Venus will retrograde. Set Voyager to this date and investigate the motion of Venus by following the above instructions for Mars.

Project Result 5:   Printout of Venus' retrograde motion and the **Planet Magnitudes** screen for the same year(s). Record your observations in the Venus Retrograde Motion table of the project report.

Project Report 18

Backing It Up

Name_____ Student Number_____

Project Goal:

PROJECT RESULTS

1. Printout of Mars' retrograde motion 1990

2. Mars retrograde motion 1990 table

Date	Phase (% Illum.)	App. Mag.	Ang. Size	Dist. (AU)	Time Rising	Setting
08/11/1990						
11/24/1990						
02/23/1991						

3. Printout of the Planet Magnitudes screen for Mars' 1990 retrograde motion. Based on your printouts and the above table,

A. Describe the observed change in **apparent brightness** and explain the reason for this change.

B. Describe the observed change in **angular size** and explain the reason for this change.

C. Date of opposition _____

D. Date of beginning retrograde _____

E. Date of ending retrograde _____

F. Duration of retrograde motion _____

4. Printout of Mars' retrograde motion for the year_____

5. Venus' retrograde motion for the year_____

A. Printout of Venus' retrograde motion 199?

B. Venus retrograde motion 199? table

Date	Phase (% Illum.)	App. Mag.	Ang. Size	Dist. (AU)	Time Rising	Setting

C. Printout of the **Planet Magnitudes** screen for the year that Venus retrogrades. Based on your printouts and the above table,

(1) Describe the observed change in **apparent brightness** and explain the reason for this change.

(2) Describe the observed change in **angular size** and explain the reason for this change.

(3) Date of inferior conjunction _____

(4) Date of beginning retrograde _____

(5) Date of ending retrograde _____

(6) Duration of retrograde motion _____

C. Venus' angular size is the largest when it appears (brightest, faintest). Why?

D. On about what date after the first retrograde motion will Venus again retrograde? _____

E. Approximately how often does Venus retrograde?_____

F. The synodic period of Venus is _____.

Conclusions and Comments

PROJECT 19

A Different Point of View

GOAL: TO OBSERVE THE EARTH'S RETROGRADE MOTION FROM MARS

INTRODUCTION

From the Earth's point of view Mercury and Venus are the inferior planets while the superior planets are those from Mars outward. But from the point of view of Mars, the inferior planets are Mercury, Venus, and the Earth while the superior planets are those from Jupiter outward. In previous projects you have learned about the phases and retrograde motion of the planets as seen from the Earth. Seen from Mars the planets also retrograde and go through phases with the inferior planets exhibiting the same phases as the Moon and the superior planets having only full and gibbous phases.

Because the Earth revolves around the Sun in 1 year while Mars requires 1.88 years, the faster moving Earth overtakes Mars at regular time intervals. At such times an observer on Mars would say that the Earth was at **inferior conjunction**. The Earth's **synodic period** would be the time between two of these inferior conjunctions.

SET LOCATION AND TIME

Pull down the **Control** menu to **Set Location** and use **Major Cities** to set your location at **London**. Then,

- ❑ **Control@Set Time@Universal Time**
- ❑ **Dialog**
  08/11/1990
  5:00 P.M.
- ❑ **Double Click or OK or Return**

THE EARTH'S RETROGRADE MOTION

With the aid of Voyager you can observe the Earth's retrograde motion from Mars.

- ❑ **Control@Sky View@Solar System**
- ❑ **Options@Track Planets**
- ❑ **Options@Observe From Planet@Mars**
- ❑ **Objects Off**
- ❑ **Earth On**
- ❑ **Center Earth**
- ❑ **Lock Earth**
- ❑ **Time Step 1 week**
- ❑ **Path On**
- ❑ **Forward**

Project Result 1: Starting on 08/11/1990 view the complete retrograde motion of the Earth and make a white sky printout of this motion.

Project Result 2: Reset the date to 08/11/1990. Click on the Earth to bring up its information box. Record the information requested in the Earth Retrograde Motion 1990 table of the project report and use **Forward** or **Set Time** to advance Earth's position to the next date in the table.

As the distance between the Earth and Mars changes, the apparent brightness and angular size of the Earth also change. The **Planet Magnitudes** command plots the changing magnitude (small dots) and angular size (large dots) of a planet as viewed from the Mars. The buttons at the bottom of the screen allow you to plot this data for each of the three listed years. The **Print Magnitudes** command will print the displayed graph.

- ❑ **Options@Planet Magnitudes**
- ❑ **Click Year Button**
- ❑ **Click Earth Box**
- ❑ **File@Print Magnitudes**

Project Result 3: Make a printout of the Planet Magnitudes screen for the year(s) that the Earth retrogrades and discuss the reason for the observed changes in brightness and angular size. It is very important to remember that the smaller the magnitude the brighter the object.

Project Result 4: Make a printout showing the Earth's retrograde motion at its next inferior conjunction.

THE EARTH'S PHASES

Viewed from Mars the Earth goes through phases. To observe these phases,

- ❑   **Display@Major Planets@Planet Images**
- ❑   **Dialog**
     Earth Disk On
- ❑   **OK or Return**
- ❑   **Display@Black Sky**
- ❑   **Center Earth**
- ❑   **Lock Earth**
- ❑   **Zoom in to disk**
- ❑   **Forward**

Project Result 5: Watch the Earth go through at least one full cycle of phases and record your observations in the project report.

Project Report 19

A Different Point of View

Name_____   Student Number_____

Project Goal:

PROJECT RESULTS

1. Printout of Earth's retrograde motion 1990

2. Earth retrograde motion 1990 table

Date	Phase (% Illum.)	App. Mag.	Ang. Size	Dist. (AU)
08/11/1990				
11/24/1990				
02/23/1991				

3. Printout of the **Planet Magnitudes** screen for the Earth's 1990 retrograde motion. Based on your printouts and the above table,

> **A.** Describe the observed change in **apparent brightness** and explain the reason for this change.

B. Describe the observed change in **angular size** and explain the reason for this change.

C. Date of inferior conjunction _____

D. Date of beginning retrograde _____

E. Date of ending retrograde _____

F. Duration of retrograde motion _____

G. Synodic period of Earth _____

Hint: Viewed from the Earth the synodic period of Mars is 2.1 years.

4. Printout of the Earth's retrograde motion for the year_____

5. The Earth's phases viewed from Mars

A. What phases did the Earth go through?

B. In what phase was the Earth's angular size largest?_____

C. What phase did the Earth exhibit when it began to retrograde? _____

(1) Was it closest to Mars at this time?_____

(2) Was it brightest at this time? Explain.

Conclusions and Comments

Chapter 9

Satellite and Ring Systems

The Medicean Stars

GOAL: TO OBSERVE JUPITER'S MOONS AND LEARN ABOUT GALILEO'S FIRST TELESCOPIC OBSERVATIONS OF THESE MOONS

Galileo Galilei (1564 - 1642)

Galileo, born in Pisa and raised in Florence, Italy, lived a long, turbulent, but highly productive life. He challenged the scientific and religious authority of his time and paved the way for a new observational astronomy as well as a new physics. His telescopic discovery of Jupiter's moons convinced him that the Copernican system was correct and eventually led to his 1633 trial before the Inquisition. As a result of the trial Galileo was made to denounce his beliefs and was sentenced to house arrest in his villa outside of Florence for the rest of his life. Ironically, this far-sighted scientist, who had enlarged the universe a thousand fold, died in 1642 totally blind and confined to the space of his villa. As fate would have it, Isaac Newton was born Christmas day of the same year.

On September 25, 1608, many years before Galileo's tragic end, a Dutch eyeglass maker by the name of Hans Lippershey applied for a patent on "a certain device by means of which all things at a very great distance can be seen as if they were nearby. " But Lippershey was not given a patent because the government officials in the newly formed Dutch Republic felt that the new device could be too easily copied. Indeed, the telescope was already being sold by a Dutch peddler at a yearly autumn fair in Frankfurt, Germany.

Galileo first heard the rumor of the new Dutch invention in May 1609. He immediately obtained some lenses and made his own telescope having a magnification of three times. Over the next few months, by trial and error, he tripled the magnification and donated the instrument to the Venetian Republic. By giving the Venetian Senate the sole right to manufacture this telescope Galileo hoped to improve his position at the state supported University of Padua where he had been teaching mathematics since 1592. His contract at the university was, in fact, renewed for life and his salary doubled. However, much to his disappointment he later found that his new contract excluded further salary increases.

Perhaps hoping to improve his position by improving the telescope, Galileo increased the magnification to 20 times and began observing the heavens. He first directed the new instrument at the Moon, writing in a January 7, 1610 letter,

> ... it is seen that the Moon is most evidently not at all of an even, smooth, and regular surface, as a great many people believe of it and of other heavenly bodies, but on the contrary it is rough and unequal. In short it is shown to be such that sane reasoning cannot conclude otherwise than that it is full of prominences and cavities similar, but much larger, to the mountains and valleys spread over the Earth's surface.[1]

Not all planets were favorably placed for viewing at the beginning of January 1610. Saturn and Mars were located in the sky close to the Sun and at their greatest distance from the Earth while Venus was in the morning sky. But Galileo still noticed that these planets looked like small disks through his telescope. The situation was much better for Jupiter, which had just passed opposition. Rising around sunset it was the brightest object, except for the Moon, in the evening sky. In his January 7 letter Galileo mentioned for the first time that

> ... only this evening I have seen Jupiter accompanied by three fixed stars, totally invisible because of their smallness: and the configuration was in this form:

East   *   * O   *   West

By at least January 15 Galileo realized that the "stars" were not fixed at all but were revolving around Jupiter. He also recognized the great significance of this fact and knew that it would not be long before

---

[1] All quotes as well as specifics concerning dates are taken from Albert Van Helden's excellent translation of Galileo's book *Siderius Nuncius*, The University of Chicago Press, 1989. Used by permission.

others made the same discovery. He therefore decided to write a book describing his observations. But being politically astute, he first wrote a letter describing his discoveries to Cosimo de Medici, an ex-pupil, who had become the Grand Duke Cosimo II of Tuscany. Galileo soon heard from the Grand Duke and his three brothers who all were "astonished by this new proof of [his] almost supernatural intelligence."

On February 13 Galileo wrote to the Grand Duke's secretary,

> ... since it is up to me, the first discoverer, to name these new planets, I wish, in imitation of the ancient sages who placed the most excellent heroes of that age among the stars, to inscribe these with the name of the Most Serene Grand Duke. There only remains in me a little indecision whether I should dedicate all four to the Grand Duke only, calling them Cosmian after his name or, rather, since they are exactly four in number, dedicate them to all four brothers with the name Medicean Stars.

Much to Galileo's surprise he was informed that the Grand Duke liked the latter choice. On March 13, 1610 he sent the Grand Duke an unbound copy of his new book and six days later a bound copy along with the telescope that he had used to discover the "Medicean Stars". For the book Galileo chose the name *Sidereus Nuncius* or *The Starry Messenger*.

SET LOCATION AND TIME

Pull down the **Control** menu to **Set Location** and choose **World Map.** Enter the location of Padua, Italy at longitude 11 deg 52 min east and latitude 45 deg 24 min North. Enter the time zone as -1. Set the date to January 7, 1610 (1/07/1610) and the time to 6 P.M.

OBSERVING WITH GALILEO

The Voyager spacecraft sent back to Earth some of the most spectacular pictures ever obtained of Jupiter and its moons. With the aid of the Voyager program you can travel back in time and see these moons as Galileo saw them in the first month of the year 1610. Imagine yourself standing beside Galileo on that starry night of January 7, 1610, dressed in the clothes worn during the reign of Elizabeth I, perhaps having just read one of Shakespeare's latest plays. To set the stage,

- ❏   Control@Sky View@Local Horizon
- ❏   Options@Track Planets
- ❏   Display@Major Planets@Jupiter's Moons
- ❏   Display@Coordinate Lines@Ecliptic
- ❏   Center Jupiter
- ❏   Lock Jupiter
- ❏   Time Step 1 hour
- ❏   Constellations On

Project Result 1:

Project Result 1: Make a white sky printout of the sky. Having returned the sky to black, record your observations in The Evening Sky, January 7, 1610 of the project report.

THE STARRY MESSENGER

In *Sidereus Nuncius* Galileo reported his observations of Jupiter's moons between January 7 and March 2, 1610. He made sketches and estimated the angular separations between Jupiter and the moons.

Make sure that Jupiter is centered and locked and check that the date is January 7, 1610. Zoom in as far as you can to view the moons.

Project Result 2: Repeat Galileo's observations as described in the following excerpt from *Sidereus Nuncius* and record your observations in the project report. Leave the time set at 6 PM and change only the date using **Set Time**. To identify a moon simply click on it. After you have recorded your data reset the date to January 7, 1610 at 6 PM. Click forward and simply watch the moons until at least March 2, 1610.

Accordingly, on the seventh day of January of the present year 1610, at the first hour of the night, when I inspected the celestial constellations through a spyglass, Jupiter presented himself. And since I had prepared for myself a superlative instrument, I saw (which earlier had not happened because of the weakness of the other instruments) that three little stars were positioned near him - small but yet very bright. Although I believed them to be among the number of fixed stars, they nevertheless intrigued me because they appeared to be arranged exactly along a straight line and parallel to the ecliptic, and to be brighter than others of equal size. And their disposition among themselves and with respect to Jupiter was as follows:

East   *   * O   *   West

That is, two stars were near him on the east and one on the west; the more eastern one and the western one appeared a bit larger than the remaining one. I was not in the least concerned with their distances from Jupiter, for, as we said above, at first I believed them to be fixed stars. But when, on the eighth, I returned to the same observation, guided by I know not what fate, I found a very different arrangement. For all three little stars were to the west of Jupiter and closer to each other than the previous night, and separated by equal intervals, as shown in the adjoining sketch. Even though at this point

East   O * * *   West

I had by no means turned my thought to the mutual motions of these stars, yet I was aroused by the question of how Jupiter could be to the east of all the said fixed stars when the day before he had been to the west of two of them. I was afraid, therefor, that perhaps, contrary to the astronomical computations, his motion was direct and that, by his proper motion, he had bypassed those stars. For this reason I waited eagerly for the next night. But I was disappointed in my hope, for the sky was everywhere covered with clouds.

Then, on the tenth, the stars appeared in this position with regard to Jupiter. Only two stars were near him, both to the east. the third, as I thought, was hidden behind Jupiter. As before,

East   *   * O   West

they were in the same straight line with Jupiter and exactly aligned along the zodiac. When I saw this, and since I knew that such changes could in no way be assigned to Jupiter, and since I knew, moreover, that the observed stars were always the same ones (for no others, either preceding or following Jupiter, were present along the zodiac for a great distance), now, moving from doubt to astonishment, I found that the observed change was not in Jupiter but in the said stars. And so, on the eleventh, I saw the following arrangement:

East   * *   O   West

There were only two stars on the east, of which the middle one was three times as far from Jupiter than from the more eastern one, and the more eastern one was about twice as large as the other, although the previous night they had appeared about equal. I therefore arrived at the conclusion, entirely beyond doubt, that in the heavens there are three stars wandering around Jupiter like Venus and Mercury around the Sun. This was at length seen clear as day in many subsequent observations, and also that there are not only three, but four wandering stars making their revolutions about Jupiter. The following is an account of the changes in their positions, accurately determined from then on. I also measured the distances between them with the glass, by the procedure explained above. I have added the times of the observations, especially when more than one were made on the same night, for the revolutions of these planets are so swift that the hourly differences can often be perceived as well.

Thus, on the twelfth, at the first hour of the following night, I saw the stars arranged in this manner.

East   * * O *   West

The more eastern star was larger than the western one, but both were very conspicuous and bright. Both were two minutes distant from Jupiter.

Project Result 3:
Set Voyager to your present location, time, and date and make a white sky printout. If Jupiter is below your horizon either change the time or view Jupiter using **Star Atlas**. Label the moons. Record your observations of Jupiter's moons in Jupiter's Moons Today in the project report. Click forward and watch the moons as they revolve.

Project Report 20

The Medicean Stars

Name_____ Student Number_____

Project Goal:

PROJECT RESULTS

1. The evening sky, January 7, 1610

A. Printout of sky

B. The Moon's

Phase _____
Magnitude _____
Rising time _____
Setting time _____
Angular distance from Jupiter _____

C. Jupiter's

Phase _____
Magnitude _____
Rising time _____
Setting time _____

D. Do you think the Moon may have hindered Galileo's observations of Jupiter? Why or why not?

E. On this evening where would Galileo have looked for Saturn?

F. Could Galileo have observed Mars and Venus early on the evening of January 7? If so where, if not why not?

2. *The Starry Messenger*

For each of the following dates sketch and identify Jupiter's moons. If Galileo estimated angular separations indicate your measurement. For various reasons Galileo did not always see all of the visible moons. When your observations differ from Galileo's, point out the differences and suggest a reason for these differences. You can measure the angular separation between any two objects by clicking on each object and then choosing **Angular Separation** from the **Field** menu.

A. Were the moons parallel to the ecliptic as Galileo observed?

B. January 7, 1610

     East   O   West

     Angular separation_____

     Observed differences:

C. January 8, 1610

     East   O   West

     Angular separation_____

     Observed differences:

D. January 9, 1610 was cloudy, but had Galileo been able to observe he would have seen

East   O   West

Angular separation_____

E. January 10, 1610

East   O   West

Angular separation_____

Observed differences:

F. January 11, 1610

East   O   West

Angular separation_____

Observed differences:

G. January 12, 1610

East   O   West

Angular separation_____

Observed differences:

3.   Jupiter's moons today

    A. Printout with moons labeled

    B. Location and time

            Longitude _____
            Latitude _____
            Date _____
            Time _____

    C. Jupiter's

            Phase _____
            Magnitude _____
            Rising time _____
            Setting time _____

    D. Labeled sketch of moons

East   O   West

Conclusions and Comments

PROJECT 21

Lords of the Rings

GOAL: TO OBSERVE THE RING SYSTEMS OF SATURN AND OTHER PLANETS

INTRODUCTION

In January of 1610, Saturn was close to the Sun and setting in the early evening. It was not well placed for observation. With his newly improved telescope Galileo was able to see little about this planet except that it looked like a small disk. But in July Saturn was visible throughout the evening and Galileo discovered that it seemed to have a peculiar appearance. He wrote to the secretary of the Grand Duke Cosimo II of Tuscany:

> [T]he star Saturn is not a single one, but an arrangement of three that almost touch each other and never move or change with respect to each other; and they are placed on a line along the zodiac, the one in the middle being about three times larger than the other two on the sides; and they are situated in this form oOo [.] [1]

Galileo's best telescopes were unable to show Saturn's rings which appeared as he drew them in his letter. The strange appearance of Saturn was not resolved until 1655 when Christian Huygens established that a ring system encircled the planet.

Ground based telescopes reveal three obvious rings with what appear to be dark gaps between some of the rings. The Voyager spacecraft sent back to Earth some of the most detailed pictures ever obtained of the rings of Saturn. These pictures show that the three major rings are themselves made up of hundreds of thousands of

---

[1] From Albert Van Helden's translation of Galileo's book *Siderius Nuncius*, The University of Chicago Press, 1989. Used by permission.

"ringlets." The rings are composed of smallish particles orbiting about Saturn in a very thin disk.

GALILEO'S SATURN

Pull down the **Control** menu to **Set Location** and choose **World Map.** Enter the location of Padua, Italy at longitude 11 deg 52 min east and latitude 45 deg 24 min north. Enter the time zone as minus one (-1). Set the date to July 13, 1610 (7/13/1610) and the time to 10 P.M.

- ❑ **Control Menu@Sky View@Local Horizon**
- ❑ **Options@Track Planets**
- ❑ **Center Saturn**
- ❑ **Lock Saturn**
- ❑ **Display@Major Planets@Rings of Saturn, Uranus, and Neptune On**
- ❑ **Display@Major Planets@Planet Images**
- ❑ **Dialog**
  Disks of Saturn, Uranus, and Neptune On
- ❑ **OK or Return**
- ❑ **Zoom in**

Project Result 1: Record your observations of Saturn in the project report.

RINGS AROUND THE PLANETS

Astronomers now know that even Jupiter, Uranus, and Neptune have ring systems, although these ring systems are not nearly as fascinating as the fabulous rings of Saturn. Set the date to July 13, 1990 at 10 P.M. **Center** Saturn and **Zoom in**.

Project Result 2: Record your observations in the Rings Around the Planets section of the project report. Make a white screen printout. Repeat for Uranus and Neptune. Leave the zoom setting the same for all three planets. Then by centering each planet you can rapidly switch between planets and compare their apparent sizes.

AN EARTH TRANSIT OF THE SUN

On 14 July 1990, if you were observing from Saturn, you would be able to watch a solar transit of the Earth. With the aid of Voyager you can do just that.

- ❑ Options@Observe From Planet@Saturn
- ❑ Center Sun
- ❑ Lock Sun
- ❑ Time Step 2 hours and click
- ❑ Zoom In
- ❑ Forward

Project Result 3: Answer the questions under An Earth Transit of the Sun in the project report.

THE CHANGING ASPECT OF SATURN'S RINGS

The orientation of Saturn's rings is continuously changing. To watch this change,

- ❑ Options@Return to Earth
- ❑ Control Menu@Sky View@Star Atlas
- ❑ Center Saturn
- ❑ Lock Saturn
- ❑ Zoom In
- ❑ Time Step 1 month
- ❑ Forward

Project Result 4: Watch the changing aspect of Saturn's rings over a period of at least ten years and answer the questions under The Changing Aspect of Saturn's Rings in the project report.

Project Report 21

Lords of the Rings

Name_____ Student Number_____

Project Goal:

PROJECT RESULTS

1. Galileo's Saturn, July 13, 1610

Phase _____
Magnitude _____
Distance from Earth _____
Apparent size _____
Rising time _____
Setting time _____

2. Rings around the planets, July 13, 1990

A. Saturn printout

Phase _____
Magnitude _____
Distance from Earth _____
Apparent size _____
Rising time _____
Setting time _____

B. Uranus Printout   **C.** Neptune Printout

Phase _____   Phase _____
Magnitude _____   Magnitude _____
Distance from Earth _____   Distance from Earth _____
Apparent size _____   Apparent size _____
Rising time _____   Rising time _____
Setting time _____   Setting time _____

D. What would account for the difference in the apparent sizes of the planets?

E. What is different about the appearance of Uranus' rings?

3. An Earth transit of the Sun

A. Earth data

Phase _____
Magnitude _____
Distance from Saturn _____
Apparent size _____

B. What would be the phase of Saturn as viewed from Earth during the transit? _____.

4. The Changing aspect of Saturn's rings

A. On what date did Saturn's rings seem to disappear? _____

B. Explain why the rings seemed to disappear.

Conclusions and Comments

Chapter 10

Magnitudes and the H-R Diagram

Project 22 Star Light Star Bright

The Inverse Square Law of Light and
Magnitude Systems

Project 23 Great Balls of Fire

Giants, Dwarfs, and the H-R Diagram

PROJECT 22

Star Light Star Bright

GOAL: TO LEARN ABOUT THE INVERSE SQUARE LAW OF LIGHT AND MAGNITUDE SYSTEMS

THE INVERSE SQUARE LAW

We are all familiar with the fact that at night the headlights of an approaching car appear brighter as they get nearer. From experience we feel that fainter corresponds to farther.   How bright a light source seems, the **apparent brightness**, does indeed depend on the distance. However, it also depends on how bright the source actually is. This **intrinsic brightness** is related to the amount of energy that the source is emitting. The apparent brightness may also depend on the presence of intervening material. For example, approaching headlights seem fainter when there is fog.

Disregarding the latter complication, the **inverse square law** of light states that the apparent brightness, b, is directly proportional to the intrinsic brightness, B, and inversely proportional to the distance, D, squared,

$$b \sim B/D^2$$

To illuminate this law, consider 60 and 120 watt light bulbs placed at the same distance. The 120 watt bulb is intrinsically twice as bright as the 60 watt bulb and will therefore appear to be twice as bright. If the distance to the bulbs is doubled, both will appear only one-fourth as bright. Removed to three times the original distance their apparent brightness becomes only one ninth as great. On the other hand, if the 120 watt bulb were placed twice as far away as the 60 watt bulb it would appear to be one half as bright as the 60 watt bulb. As another example, the Sun is the brightest star in our sky. But if we could view the Sun from thirty times farther out, it would appear to be only one-nine hundredth (1/900) as bright. The Sun appears bright not because it is intrinsically brighter than other stars but because it is so very much closer.

THE MAGNITUDE SYSTEM

In the second century B.C. the Greek astronomer Hipparchus grouped the stars visible to the naked eye into six brightness categories. The apparently brightest stars he called first magnitude stars, the next, second magnitude stars, and so on to the just barely visible sixth magnitude stars. The numbers assigned to stars based on their apparent brightness are known as **apparent magnitudes**. Astronomers today use an extended version of Hipparchus' system. With telescopes it is possible to detect very faint stars having magnitudes of around +27. At the bright end of the magnitude scale is the Sun with an apparent magnitude of about -27. Notice that very bright stars have large **negative** magnitudes while very faint stars have large **positive** magnitudes. One of the closer stars, Alpha Centauri, has a magnitude of 0 right at the center of the magnitude scale. The apparent brightness of other objects such as planets and comets can also be expressed in terms of magnitudes.

Since apparent magnitudes depend on distance, they cannot be used to compare the intrinsic brightness of objects unless their distances are known. Sometimes it is convenient to imagine all stars being at the same distance. If this were the case apparent brightness would be a true indication of an object's intrinsic brightness. Astronomers define **absolute magnitude** as the apparent magnitude that an object would have if it were at a distance of 10 parsecs. A **parsec** (pc) is 3.26 light years (l.yr.) or approximately 19.6 trillion miles.

The human eye perceives brightness in such a way that a difference of one magnitude corresponds to a factor of 2.512 in brightness. That is, a first magnitude object is 2.512 times brighter than a second magnitude object, and a second magnitude object is 2.512 times brighter than a third. A difference of two magnitudes, however, corresponds to a factor of 2.512 times 2.512, or as it is often expressed, 2.512^2. Thus, a first magnitude star is 2.512^2 or 6.31 times brighter than a third magnitude star. A difference of three magnitudes is a factor of 2.512^3.

The relationship between magnitude difference and apparent brightness can be expressed as a **brightness ratio**,

$$b_n/b_m = 2.512^{(m-n)}$$

where b_n and b_m are the apparent brightness of objects having apparent magnitudes n and m, respectively. For example, the brightness ratio for a first and third magnitude object is $b_1/b_3 = 2.512^{(3-1)} = 2.512^2$. The magnitude difference between the apparently brightest object, the Sun, and the faintest observable object is 54 magnitudes. The corresponding brightness ratio is

$$b_{-27}/b_{27} = 2.512^{54}$$

This is truly an astronomically large range in the brightness of observable objects.

The intrinsic brightnesses of two objects can also be compared using the above formula. In this case the brightness ratio would be written as

$$B_M/B_N = 2.512^{(N-M)}$$

where B_M and B_N are the intrinsic brightnesses of objects having absolute magnitudes M and N. If one of the two objects is the Sun,

$$B_M/B_{Sun} = 2.512^{(4.8-M)}$$

where 4.8 is the Sun's absolute magnitude.

You intuitively judge the distance of approaching headlights at night by comparing how bright they appear with your knowledge of how bright the headlights should be. That is, you compare the apparent brightness and the intrinsic brightness of the headlights. Astronomers do the same sort of thing using the inverse square law of light. The absolute magnitude, M, is a measure of the intrinsic brightness while the apparent magnitude, m, is related to the apparent brightness. Using the inverse square law and the expression for brightness ratio it is possible to show that the distance of an object is

$$D = 10 \times 2.512^{0.5(m-M)} \ parsecs$$

The difference between apparent and absolute magnitudes, m-M, is called the **distance modulus.** If the distance modulus is known, the distance to the star can be computed.

SET LOCATION AND TIME

Pull down the **Control** menu to **Set Location** and use either **Major Cities** or **World Map** to set the longitude and latitude of your location. You need not worry about setting the date. Use the values that Voyager has entered. But set the time to **12 noon**.

THE SUN'S APPARENT MAGNITUDE

With Voyager you can place yourself on any planet and determine how bright the Sun looks.

- ❑ Sky View@Star Atlas
- ❑ Field@Center On Planet@Sun
- ❑ Options@Observe From Planet@Mercury

Project Result 1: Click on the Sun to open its information box and note the Sun's distance from Mercury and the Sun's apparent magnitude as seen from Mercury. Observe the Sun from the other planets and record its magnitude and distance in the project report.

THE SOLAR NEIGHBORHOOD

Choose **Solar Neighborhood** from the **Options** menu. A window will appear showing the 60 stars nearest the Sun. You are observing from a distance of 50 light years, looking back towards the Sun at the center of the display.

Project Result 2: For a number of stars brighter than fifth magnitude record the data requested in the tables of the project report. Compare each star's intrinsic brightness to that of the Sun by computing the brightness ratio. Repeat for a number of stars fainter than fifth magnitude.

Click on the **XYZ Axes** button and then use the arrow keys at the right of the screen to rotate the display. As the display turns you will be able to easily see the three-dimensional relationship between the Sun and its neighbors.

Project Report 22

Star Light Star Bright

Name_____   Student Number_____

Project Goal:

PROJECT RESULTS

1. The Sun's distance and apparent magnitude

View From	Sun Dist. (AU)	Inverse Sq. (Earth/Planet)^2	Sun m	Mag. Diff. (Earth - Planet)	Bright. Ratio 2.512^{diff}
Mercury					
Venus					
Earth	1.00		-26.7	0.0	0.0
Mars					
Jupiter					
Saturn					
Uranus					
Neptune					
Pluto					

Hint: The numbers in the third column for the inverse square law and in the last column for the brightness ratio should be approximately the same.

    A. How many times brighter is the Sun as seen from Mercury than it is when viewed from the Earth? _____

    B. How many times fainter is the Sun as seen from Pluto than it is when viewed from the Earth? _____

2.   The solar neighborhood

    A. Stars brighter than fifth magnitude

Star	m (<5)	M	D (l.yr.)	D (parsec)	B_M/B_{Sun}
1					
2					
3					
4					
5					
6					
7					
8					
9					
10					

B. Stars fainter than fifth magnitude

Star	m (>5)	M	D (l.yr.)	D (parsec)	B_M/B_{Sun}
1					
2					
3					
4					
5					
6					
7					
8					
9					
10					

C. Based on the above data,

(1) If a star's apparent magnitude, m, is less than its absolute magnitude, M, the star is (farther, closer) than 10 parsecs.

(2) For the apparently faint stars (m > 5) what is the average

Distance in parsecs? _____
Apparent magnitude? _____
Absolute magnitude? _____
B_M/B_{Sun} _____

(3) For the apparently bright stars (m < 5) what is the average

Distance in parsecs? _____
Apparent magnitude? _____
Absolute magnitude? _____
B_M/B_{Sun} _____

(4) What percentage of the apparently faint stars that you observed are intrinsically brighter than the Sun?

_____

(5) What percentage of the apparently bright stars that you observed are intrinsically brighter than the Sun?

_____

(6) Are the apparently brightest stars bright because they are intrinsically bright or because they are close?

Conclusions and Comments

PROJECT 23

Great Balls of Fire

GOAL: TO LEARN ABOUT THE SPECTRAL CLASSIFICATION OF STARS AND TO INVESTIGATE THE HERTZSPRUNG-RUSSELL DIAGRAM

SPECTRAL CLASSIFICATION

When sunlight is passed through a prism a band of colors, ranging from violet to red, is produced. These colors correspond to wavelengths of light between 4000 and 7000 angstroms, a unit equal to 10^{-8} centimeters. The entire solar spectrum, however, extends beyond this **visible spectrum** in both directions towards very short and very long wavelengths. The visible spectrum of the Sun and stars can be photographed with a device known as a **spectrograph**. The resulting picture is called a **spectrogram**.

The spectra of most stars are **absorption spectra**, composed of discrete dark lines produced by various atoms and ions. Some spectra also have broader bands produced by molecules. Since each atom, ion, or molecule has a unique and characteristic set of lines or bands, the chemical composition of stars can be determined. Stars can also be classified using criteria based on the appearance of the spectra.

The Draper catalog, published in 1890, was the initial effort of Harvard University astronomers to classify the varied patterns of lines and bands in stellar spectra. One of the greatest women astronomers of the time, Williamina Fleming, made monumental contributions to the development of the Draper catalog, which contained spectral classifications for 10,351 stars.

Most stars have very similar chemical compositions. They are composed primarily of hydrogen with some helium and very little of the remaining elements. The variation in the appearance of stellar spectra is therefore not due to large differences in chemical composition but rather results from a variation in the temperatures of stellar atmospheres, where the absorption spectrum is formed.

The horizontal axis of the graph in Figure 23.1 is labeled with the letters astronomers call spectral classes. Each class is subdivided into ten sub-classes designated by a number. For example, A0, A1, A2, ..., A9. Not all of spectral classes and sub-classes are shown in the figure. The vertical axis of the graph indicates the temperature in degrees Kelvin (deg K). It is obvious that the atmospheres of B0 class stars are considerably hotter than those of G2 stars such as the Sun. The coolest stars are those of spectral class M. Since the color of a star depends on its temperature, the **spectral sequence**, as the arrangement is called, is also a color sequence.

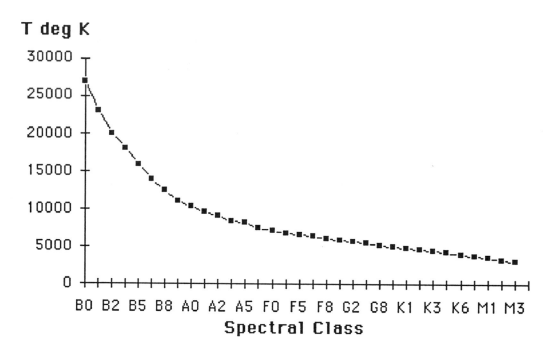

Figure 23.1 Spectral Sequence

The hottest stars, O (not shown) and B type, are blue-white, while G type stars are yellow like the Sun, and the coolest stars, M type, are red. Notice that the relationship between temperature and color is just the opposite of what everyday usage suggests, namely, "blue with cold" and "red hot"!

THE HERTZSPRUNG-RUSSELL DIAGRAM

Early in the twentieth century the Danish astronomer Ejnar Hertzsprung and the American astronomer Henry Norris Russell independently developed a diagram that is now named after them and is often referred to simply as the **H-R diagram**. This diagram, which is one of the most important in modern astronomy, is a plot of the absolute magnitude of stars versus their spectral class. Since absolute magnitude is a measure of intrinsic brightness and spectral class is related to temperature, the H-R diagram is really a plot of intrinsic brightness versus temperature. In Figure 23.2 the diagram is shown in both ways. Note that stars are located in the four areas labeled **Supergiants**, **Giants**, **Main Sequence**, and **White Dwarfs**.

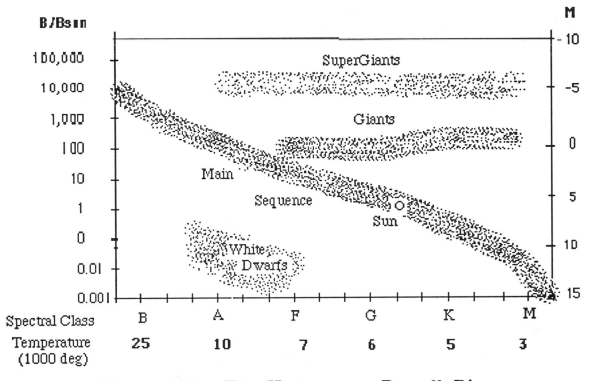

Figure 23.2   The Hertzsprung-Russell Diagram

Besides its spectral class a star is also assigned a brightness, or as it is more often called, a **luminosity class**. For example, main sequence stars belong to luminosity class V, giants to class III, supergiants to class I, and white dwarfs to Wd.

Recall that the relationship between magnitude difference and brightness can be expressed as a **brightness ratio**,

$$b_n/b_m = 2.512^{(m-n)}$$

where b_n and b_m are the brightness of objects having apparent magnitudes n and m, respectively. The intrinsic brightness of the Sun and a star can be compared using a similar formula. In this case the formula is written as

$$\text{(A)} \quad B_M/B_{Sun} = 2.512^{(4.8-M)}$$

where B_{Sun} and B_M are the intrinsic brightness of Sun and star, 4.8 is the absolute magnitude of the Sun, and M is the absolute magnitude of the star.

In addition, the intrinsic brightness, B, of a star is determined by its radius, R, and its temperature, T. The relationship between these quantities is given by the expression

$$\text{(B)} \quad B/B_{Sun} = (R/R_{Sun})^2 \times (T/T_{Sun})^4$$

where B_{Sun}, R_{Sun}, and T_{Sun} are, respectively, the intrinsic brightness, radius, and temperature of the Sun.

SET LOCATION AND TIME

Pull down the **Control Menu** to **Set Location** and use either **Major Cities** or **World Map** to set the longitude and latitude of your location. You need not worry about setting the date and time. Use the values that Voyager has entered.

PUTTING STARS IN THEIR PLACE

Information on stellar temperatures, magnitudes, and spectral classes can be obtained using Voyager. Use the **Center on Star** or **Find and Center** commands in the **Field** menu to locate the stars listed in the H-R diagram, data table of the project report. Click on each star to bring up its information box.

Project Result 1: For each star record the data requested in the H-R diagram data table of the project report.   Compare each star's intrinsic brightness to that of the Sun's by computing its light ratio.

Project Report 23

Great Balls of Fire

Name_____   Student Number_____

Project Goal:

PROJECT RESULTS

1. The H-R diagram

   A. Data table

Star	Sp./Lum. Class	Temp. (deg K)	m	M	D (l.yr.)	B_M/B_{Sun}
Spica				-3.3		
Altair				-2.2		
Fomalhaut				2.0		
Vega				0.5		
Sun	G2	5800	-26.8	4.8		
Tau Ceti				5.7		
61 Cygni				7.6		
Alpha Centauri				4.4		
Aldebaran				-0.7		
Capella				-0.6		
Pollux				1.0		
Arcturus				-0.3		
Rigel				-7.1		
Deneb				-7.1		
Betelgeuse				-5.6		
Canopus				-3.1		
Antares				-5.1		

Star	Sp./Lum. Class	Temp. (deg K)	m	M	D (l.yr.)	B_M/B_{Sun}
Sirius A				1.4		
Sirius B	Wd	20000	7.2	11.5	8.6	
Procyon A				2.6		
Procyon B	Wd	8000	10.8	13.1	11.4	

B. Based on the above data

(1) Plot each star in the following H-R diagram.

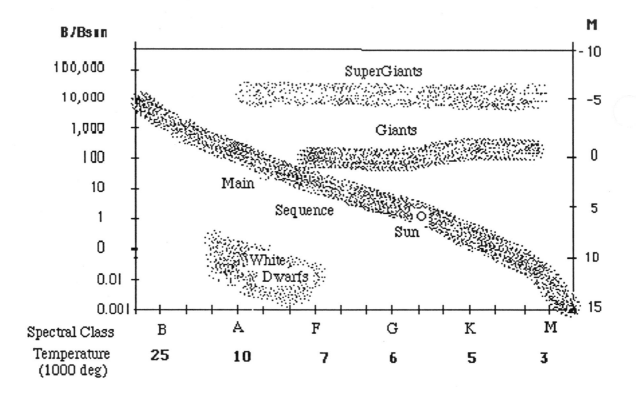

(2) Both Capella and the Sun are G type stars, having about the same surface temperature. How many times brighter is Capella than the Sun?_____

Hint: Use formula (A).

(3) Capella is _____ times larger than the Sun.

Hint: Use formula B.

(4) Capella is a type of star called a _____while the Sun is a _____.

(5)   Compared to the Sun the white dwarf

    (a) Sirius B is _____ times smaller.

    (b) Procyon B is _____ times smaller.

(6) Giant stars are intrinsically (brighter, fainter) than the Sun.

(7) White dwarfs are intrinsically (brighter, fainter) than the Sun.

(8) Class B main sequence stars are (hotter, cooler) than class M main sequence stars.

Conclusions and Comments

APPENDICES

Appendix 1   Voyager 1.2 Menu Structure

Appendix 2   Sundials

Appendix 3   Cross Staffs, Quadrants, and Gnomons

Appendix 4   Astronomical Observations

Appendix 5   Planet Data

Appendix 6   Astronomical Numbers

APPENDIX 1

Voyager 1.2 Menu Structure

MENU BAR

| File | Edit | Control | Field | Display | Options |

FILE

Load Settings ...
Save Settings→   Settings Only ...
                  Settings and Time ...
                  Orbital Data Only ....
Open Datafile ...
Show Datafile
Define Symbol ...
Page Setup ...
Print Sky Chart ...
Print Ephemeris ...
Quit

EDIT

Undo
Cut
Copy
Paste
Clear

CONTROL

Sky View→	Star Atlas
	Local Horizon
	Solar System
	Celestial Sphere
	Planetarium
	Galactic
Set Time→	Local Mean Time
	Universal Time
	Julian Day
	Use System Clock
Set Location→	World Map
	Major Cities

Magnitude Limits ...
Deep Sky Selection ...
Horizon Profile ...

Time Format→	AM-PM Clock
	24 Hour Clock
	Month/Day/Year
	Day/Month/Year
	Year/Month/Day
Precession→	2000 Epoch
	1975 Epoch
	1950 Epoch
	1900 Epoch
	Sky Panel Date
Sky Rotation→	Start Sky
	Forward
	Reverse

Sky Legend
Status
Cleanup

FIELD

Center On Constellation ...
Center On Position ...
Center On Planet➝   Sun
                       Mercury
                       Venus
                       Earth
                       Mars
                       Jupiter
                       Saturn
                       Uranus
                       Neptune
                       Pluto
                       Ceres
                       Pallas
                       Vesta
                       Juno
                       Earth's Shadow

Center On Star➝   Sirius
                       ...
                       Antares

Field and Center ...
To Current Selection
To Last Field
To Antipode
To Zenith
To Nadir
Coordinate Readouts➝   Show Readouts
                       Equatorial
                       Altazimuth
                       Ecliptic
                       Galactic

Angular Separation

DISPLAY

Major Planets→	Planet Images ...
	Planet Phases
	Planet Grids
	Earth-Moon Shadow
	Jupiter's Moons
	Rings of Saturn
	Rings of Uranus
	Rings of Neptune
Minor Planets→	Show All
	Ceres
	Pallas
	Vesta
	Juno
	Hide All
	Show As Stars
	Tails Of Comets
Messier Objects	
Variable Stars	
Binary Stars	
Grid Type→	Coarse
	Medium
	Fine
	Equatorial
	Altazimuth
	Ecliptic
	Galactic
	Number Grid
Horizon Type→	Standard
	Custom
	Transparent
	Opaque
Coordinate Lines→	Ecliptic
	Meridian
	Horizon Line
	Celestial Equator
	Galactic Equator

Reference Points→	Zenith
	Cardinal Points
	Celestial Poles
	Ecliptic Poles
	Galactic Poles
	Galactic Center
Constellation Names	
Zodiacal Constellations	
Hide Stars	
White Sky	

OPTIONS

Track Planets	
Observe From Planet→	Sun
	Mercury
	Venus
	Earth
	Mars
	Jupiter
	Saturn
	Uranus
	Neptune
	Pluto
	Ceres
	Pallas
	Vesta
	Juno
Observe From Point ...	
Return To Earth	
Define New Orbit ...	
Orbital Data	
Orrery	
Planet Positions	
Planet Magnitudes	
Conjunction Search ...	
Precession Cycle	
Solar Neighborhood	
Sky Plot	

APPENDIX 2

Sundials

BUILDING A SUNDIAL

You can use the data in the following table to construct your own sundial. The numbers in this table were computed from the formula

$$\tan D = \tan t \sin L$$

where L is the observer's latitude, D is the angle which the hour line makes with the 12 noon line, and t is the time measured from noon in angular units.

Table A2.1 Horizontal Sundial Data

Time			t (deg)	D (deg)
12 noon			0.0	0.0000
A.M.		P.M.		
11:30	or	12:30	7.5	5.0618
11:00	or	1:00	15.0	10.2193
10:30	or	1:30	22.5	15.5722
10:00	or	2:00	30.0	21.2281
9:39	or	2:30	37.5	27.3053
9:00	or	3:00	45.0	33.9325
8:30	or	3:30	52.5	41.2445
8:00	or	4:00	60.0	49.3660
7:30	or	4:30	67.5	58.3811
7:00	or	5:00	75.0	68.2845
6:30	or	5:30	82.5	78.9283
6:00	or	6:00	90.0	90.0000
5:30	or	6:30	97.5	-78.9283
5:00	or	7:00	105.0	-68.2845
4:30	or	7:30	112.5	-58.3811

1. Cut out an 8" x 7" piece of cardboard. Draw a line lengthwise down the center of the rectangle. Cut a 4 inch slot along the middle of that line. Mark one end of the cardboard North and the other end South. This is the base of your sundial (See Figure A2.1).

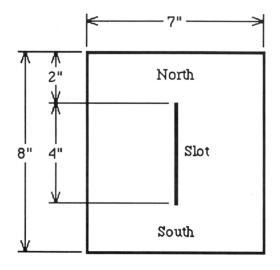

Figure A2.1 Base

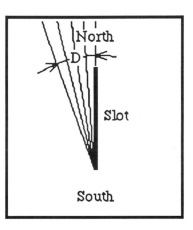

Figure A2.2 Measuring Angles

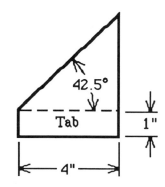

Figure A2.3 Gnomon

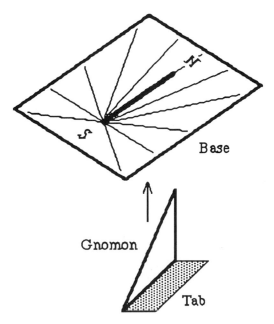

Figure A2.4 Assembly

2. Mark the south end of the slot with an X. All the hour lines will meet at this point. Measure the angles D, from the table, with the center mark of your protractor at the point labeled X. Due north is zero degrees (see Figure A2.2). Draw hour lines on both sides of the slot.

3. Cut out the gnomon as shown in Figure A2.3 and insert the gnomon through the slot in the base. Fold the tab 90 degrees and tape the tab underneath. Be sure the angled edge of the gnomon touches the X on the base (see Figure A2.4).

4. Label the hour lines on that side with the A.M. times. Label the other side with P.M. times.

> **Note:** The sundial at the end of this appendix (Figure A2.5) is both a horizontal and a vertical south-facing dial that may be cut out and mounted to a piece of cardboard. This sundial is provided for those who wish to construct a more elaborate sundial for future use. But you should try making and using your own horizontal dial.

USING THE SUNDIAL

Before using the sundial to tell time you must make sure that:

1. The base is level.
2. The gnomon is perpendicular to the base.
3. It is pointing due north.

To accomplish the latter, first decide what time you want to set up the dial. If you are in the Eastern Standard time zone your watch is reading EST. Assuming that your longitude is 5 hr 35 min west, then

$$\textbf{LMT = EST - 35 min}$$

You may choose any date and EST time for setting up the dial, say for example, an EST of 12 hr. The corresponding LMT is

$$\textbf{LMT = 12 hr - 35 min}$$
$$\textbf{or}$$
$$\textbf{LMT = 11 hr 25 min}$$

From the equation of time it follows that

$$LAT = LMT + E$$

Hence, on say, March 21 when E is -7.1 minutes (see Table 3.1) the LAT corresponding to EST noon will be

$$LAT = 11 \text{ hr } 25 \text{ min } - 7.1 \text{ min}$$
$$\text{or}$$
$$LAT = 11 \text{ hr } 17.9 \text{ min}$$

At an EST of 12 hr you would position your dial so that it was reading an LAT of 11 hr 17.9 min. By so doing you would align the dial north-south.

In short, to set up your dial choose a date and time. Then before going outside

(a) compute LMT = EST - 35 min
(b) compute LAT = LMT + E

Take the dial outside on the chosen date and time and

(c) level the dial
(d) position the dial to read the computed LAT

SUNDIAL ACTIVITY

On any clear day go out and set up your sundial. During a several hour period record the EST and the corresponding LAT on the Observation Record table. Also compute and record the corresponding LMT.

OBSERVATION RECORD

OBSERV.	DATE	EST	E	Computed LMT	Computed LAT	Observed LAT	EO
1							
2							
3							
4							
5							

Key

E = Error in Time

EO = Error in Observation

EQUATIONS

1. LMT = EST - 35 min
2. LAT = LMT + E
3. EO = LAT Comp. - LAT Observ.

NOTE: Eastern Daylight Time (EDT) - 1 Hour = Eastern Standard Time (EST)

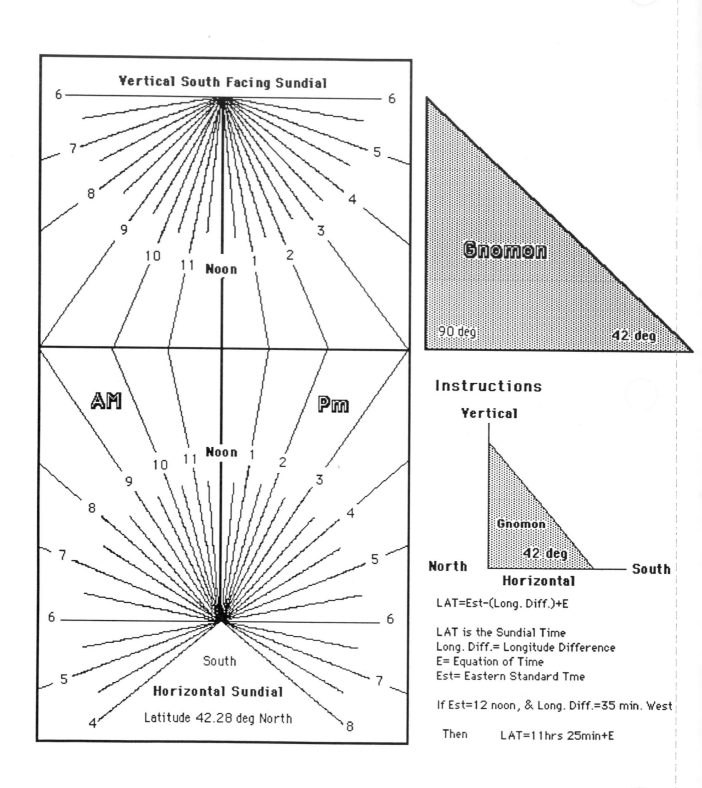

FIGURE A5 Combination Horizontal and Vertical Sundial

APPENDIX 3

Cross Staffs, Quadrants, and Gnomons

CROSS STAFFS

When you look into the night sky, it is not obvious that you are looking through thousands, millions, billions, or trillions of miles of space. It is impossible to perceive the three-dimensional arrangement of celestial objects in what appears to be the dome of the sky. A first step in understanding the night sky is to understand what your eye actually sees.

If you see someone holding an object, you compare the object's angular size to the person's angular size, and using previous knowledge of the person's height, you effortlessly estimate the object's actual size. Similarly, you estimate the actual size of the letters on this page from their angular size. In the everyday world of people, objects, and buildings, you subconsciously convert angular size into an actual size.

In the sky, however, there are no everyday objects and comprehensible distances, and you cannot perform calculations of this sort without taking measurements. But the relationships between angular size, actual size, and distance are the same.

While pointing out constellations it is no help to say "look for a star an inch, or a mile, or 20 light years, to the left of that bright one." You should say, "look 10 degrees to the left of that bright star." Likewise, while the Moon is about 2,000 miles across, how large does it look? One-half inch? Three feet? The correct answer is one-half degree. Your eye perceives **angular size.**

The cross staff is a simple device for measuring angles. It is very much like the more familiar protractor also used for measuring angles. A protractor is generally small, measures angles up to 180 degrees and is viewed from above. A cross staff is made larger to improve accuracy, measures only a few degrees, and is viewed from the vertex of the angle measured (see Figure A3.1).

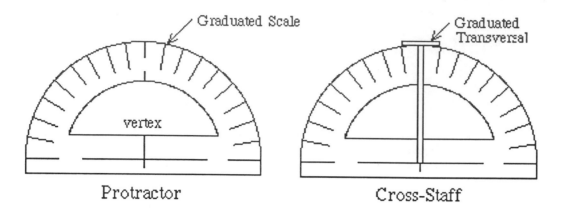

Figure A3.1   Protractor and Cross Staff

To use a cross staff, close one eye and place the end of the cross staff near the other eye. You can read the angular size, in degrees, from the **transversal**. In Figure A3.2, two stars have an angular separation of 3 degrees + 9 degrees = 12 degrees.

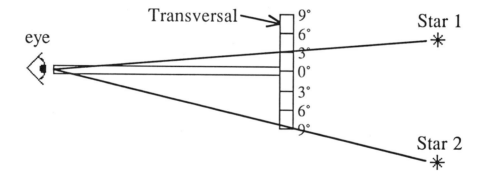

Figure A3.2   Using the Cross Staff

You can use a dowel, plastic ruler, or yardstick for the sighting arm and a second ruler or something similar for the transversal, which must be at right angles to the sighting arm. To determine the angles on the transversal you first draw, scaled down if necessary, the length of the sighting arm and transversal on a piece of paper. Second, place a protractor so that the zero line lies along the arm with the vertex mark at the eye end of the arm. Finally draw lines outward at various angles to the transversal (see Figure A3.3).

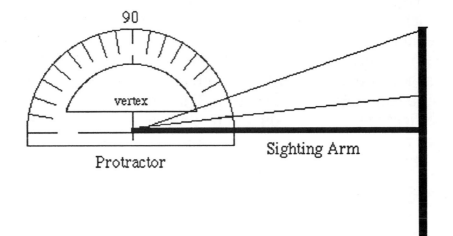

Figure A3.3   Making a Cross Staff

QUADRANTS

The quadrant is one of the oldest astronomical measuring devices. Kepler used a large quadrant, over six feet in radius, to measure the positions of the planets, and from these measurements he deduced his three laws of planetary motion.

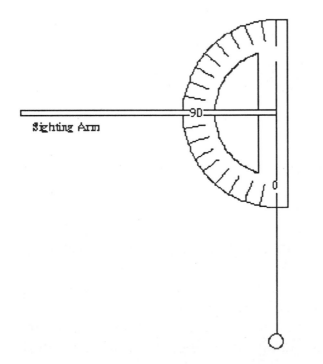

Figure A3.4   Quadrant

The word *quadrant* comes from the 90 degree arc that is used in this instrument for measuring angles. One can use a protractor, as large as possible, and a dowel or something similar for the sighting arm (see Figure A3.4). A string with a weight on one end, known as a plumb line, is attached at the vertex of the protractor. The quadrant is pointed at an object by sighting along the arm. Since the plumb line always remains vertical, defining the direction to the zenith, it will fall along the protractor at the angle corresponding to the object's altitude, 0 degrees as shown in Figure A3.4.

GNOMONS

Another ancient measuring device is the gnomon, which is nothing more than a vertical object that casts a shadow. Trees, fence posts, the sides of buildings, the stones at Stonehenge, and you, when standing in sunlight, are examples of gnomons.

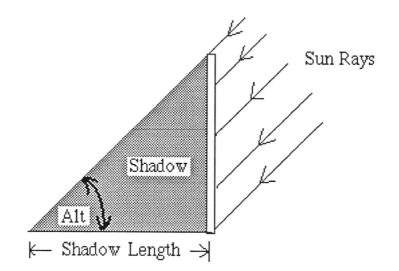

Figure A3.5   Gnomon

The altitude of the Sun is given by the expression,

tan (Alt) = height of gnomon/length of shadow

Onc can also make a scale drawing of the gnomon and shadow length and measure the angle with a protractor.

ACTIVITIES

Use Voyager's **Field@Angular Separation** command to measure the angular separation between a number of stars and check your results using a cross staff.

Measure the altitude of Polaris and a few other stars with a quadrant. You might want to observe at least one star starting when it is still to the east of your meridian and continue your observations until the star is to the west of the meridian. For each observation record the altitude and the time. A plot of altitude versus time will allow you to determine the time of upper transit and the corresponding altitude. Since altitude at upper transit is equal to 90 degrees - latitude + declination you can deduce either the star's declination or your latitude, depending on which one of these two quantities you already know. Check your results using Voyager.

You can use the gnomon to measure the Sun's altitude at upper transit following the above procedure. If you keep track of the Sun's noon altitude over a number of days, weeks, or months you will find that it changes. What information can you deduce from such observations? Check your conclusions using Voyager.

APPENDIX 4

Astronomical Observations

INTRODUCTION

Today many astronomical observations are made with space age technology, but with Voyager and simple observations using various small telescopes, binoculars, and even your unaided eye you can learn a great deal. Make as many observations over as long a time period as you can. Before you observe, make a plan for your observing and use Voyager to prepare maps to help you identify objects such as planets, stars, the Moon, meteors, and constellations. Each observation should include the name of the object observed, date, time, altitude, azimuth, right ascension, declination, sky conditions, and a description of the object. The description should include items such as: color, brightness, size, type of observing equipment, and anything else that you feel is important. A drawing of the observed object should also be made in the space provided.

OBSERVING LOG

1. Object:_____   Drawing

Date: _____   Time: _____

Altitude: _____   Azimuth: _____

R.A.: _____   Declination: _____

Sky conditions:_____

_____

Description:_____

_____

_____

_____

2. Object:_____   <u>Drawing</u>

    Date: _____   Time: _____

    Altitude: _____   Azimuth: _____

    R.A.: _____   Declination: _____

    Sky conditions:_____

    _____

    Description:_____

    _____

    _____

    _____

3. Object:_____   <u>Drawing</u>

    Date: _____   Time: _____

    Altitude: _____   Azimuth: _____

    R.A.: _____   Declination: _____

    Sky conditions:_____

    _____

    Description:_____

    _____

    _____

    _____

4. Object:_____   <u>Drawing</u>

    Date: _____   Time: _____

    Altitude: _____   Azimuth: _____

    R.A.: _____   Declination: _____

    Sky conditions:_____
    _____

    Description:_____
    _____
    _____
    _____

5. Object:_____   <u>Drawing</u>

    Date: _____   Time: _____

    Altitude: _____   Azimuth: _____

    R.A.: _____   Declination: _____

    Sky conditions:_____
    _____

    Description:_____
    _____
    _____
    _____

APPENDIX 5

Planet Data

Object	Mass (Earth = 1)	Radius (Earth = 1)	Mean Dist. (AU)	Sidereal Period (yr)	Synodic Period (days)	e	i (deg)
Mercury	0.056	0.382	0.387	0.241	115.9	0.206	7.0
Venus	0.815	0.949	0.723	0.615	583.9	0.007	3.3
Earth	1.000	1.000	1.000	1.000	NA	0.017	0.0
Moon	0.012	0.273	384.4 (km)	27.322 (days)	29.5	0.055	5.1
Mars	0.107	0.532	1.523	1.881	779.9	0.093	1.9
Jupiter	317.893	11.27	5.202	11.86	399.0	0.048	1.3
Saturn	94.3	9.44	9.588	29.46	378.0	0.056	2.5
Uranus	14.54	3.98	19.191	84.07	370.0	0.046	0.8
Neptune	17.23	3.81	30.064	164.82	367.0	0.010	1.8
Pluto	0.0023	0.27	39.528	248.6	364.0	0.248	17.2

Note: e is the orbital eccentricity and i is the inclination of the planet's orbital plane to the ecliptic.

APPENDIX 6

Astronomical Numbers

Speed of light $c = 3.00 \times 10^{10}$ cm/sec

Gravitational constant $G = 6.67 \times 10^{-8}$ dyne cm^2/g^2

1 Angstrom $1 A = 10^{-8}$ cm

Astronomical unit $1 AU = 1.496 \times 10^{13}$ cm $= 93 \times 10^6$ miles

1 Light year 1 l.yr. $= 9.46 \times 10^{17}$ cm $= 6.32 \times 10^4$ AU

1 Parsec 1 pc $= 3.09 \times 10^{18}$ cm $= 3.26$ l.yr. $= 206265$ AU

Ordering *Voyager* Software

Voyager, The Interactive Desktop Planetarium™ (Version 1.2) is available directly from Carina Softare.

For information about pricing, availability, educational site licenses, and volume discounts, contact the Educational Sales department at the following address:

Carina Software
830 Williams Street
San Leandro, CA 94577
(510) 352-7328